I am your JESUS of MERCY

Lessons and Messages
To The World
from
Our Lord and Our Lady

Published by
THE RIEHLE FOUNDATION
P.O. BOX 7
MILFORD, OHIO 45150

According to a decree of the Congregation for the Doctrine of the Faith, approved by H.H. Pope Paul VI, (1966), it is permitted to publish, without an imprimatur, texts relating to new revelations, apparitions, prophecies or miracles.

However, in accordance with the regulations of the Second Vatican Council, the publisher states that we do not wish to precede the judgment of the Church in this matter, to which we humbly submit.

Published by The Riehle Foundation
For additional copies, write:

The Riehle Foundation
P.O. Box 7
Milford, OH 45150

Copyright © 1989, The Riehle Foundation

Library of Congress Catalog Card No.: 89-063546

ISBN: 1-877678-08-2

THE RIEHLE FOUNDATION

TABLE OF CONTENTS

Publisher's Foreword

Father Jack Spaulding is a diocesan priest in the Diocese of Phoenix, Arizona. He is presently serving as a Vicar Forane in the Chancery offices there. He is also the pastor of St. Maria Goretti Parish in Scottsdale.

His commitment to his vocation and his parish is well recognized, and Father Jack is often seen on television, (EWTN), as part of the "Life Teen" program. Two years ago, Fr. Jack's commitment to youth also took him to Medjugorje with a number of young people working in the above ministry.

His parish formed a prayer group that grew to 500 people, many of them young. Its strength and commitment bore fruit. Special graces became evident. Fr. Spaulding comments on them as follows:

> "In October of 1987, a group of parishioners from St. Maria Goretti parish in Scottsdale, Arizona, made a pilgrimage to Medjugorje. The experience of Our Lord and Our Lady was very profound for these men and women, who, upon their return home, wanted to live the messages of peace, conversion, prayer, fasting, and reconciliation as best they could. On Thursday, December 3rd they began Our Lady's Prayer Group. They opened this prayerful experience up to anyone who wished to come. This group has grown from 20 to over 500 people, gathering every Thursday evening from 7 to 9 p.m., to pray the Rosary, the Chaplet of Divine Mercy, to celebrate Mass, and concluding with prayers for healing.
>
> "In July of 1988, the prayer group began receiv-

ing messages from Our Lady through one of the young adults. In December of 1988, Our Lady began speaking through me also, during the homily time of the Mass. Since then Our Lord sometimes speaks and, occasionally, gives messages through one of the young adults which are written down. During the past 10 months both a written and a spoken message from Our Lord and Our Lady are usually given.

"Since September 20, 1988, one of the young adults has been receiving Lessons from Our Lord for all of His people.

"All of these Messages and Lessons are encouraging us to allow God to become the Center of our hearts. They are words of love and concern, words of challenge and mercy, words of invitation and hope.

"The Most Reverend Thomas J. O'Brien, Bishop of the Diocese of Phoenix, has established a Commission to investigate these matters occurring at St. Maria's. As of this printing, the investigation is still in progress. The people involved are in obedience to the bishop and will follow his instructions and the findings of the Commission."

In August of 1989, Fr. Jack confided that the time had come to make these messages known to the public, in print. We feel the contents are interesting and inspiring, and appear to be an explanation of the Gospels as they apply to our lives today.

In publishing "I AM YOUR JESUS OF MERCY," we believe that this IS the time of "Divine Mercy," and that we live in a world in desperate need of recognizing it. During this period where many seem to find a need to "rework the Gospels," is the real author again speaking in His own behalf? If so, are we listening?

The publication of this book is in conformity with the regulations approved by the Vatican in October, 1966, and calls for purely human credence as to the messages contained therein.

The Riehle Foundation

Part I

Lessons From Jesus Christ, Our Lord, Given For the World

Through a Messenger At
St. Maria Goretti Parish
Scottsdale, Arizona

September 1988 through September 1989

Note:

Since all the words herein are those of Our Lord, as recorded from the messenger involved, quotation marks for each lesson are eliminated.

Prologue to the Lessons

Down through the days of our story of salvation, no matter how often we turned away from the Grace He offered us, the constancy of God's love and His enduring patience have always been the background of His invitation to allow Him to be Our God. He never gives up on us. He sent us His prophets to call us back to Him; and finally He sent His own Son, begging us to give Him our hearts so that He could give us His.

From the Cross Jesus looked down the ages and was saddened to see how, for many, His death would be offered in vain. To this day His sorrow persists. We still listen to every other invitation but the One which will give us true freedom and everlasting life.

Jesus has been given permission by that same God Who loves us, and Whom we call Father, to teach us once more in our own days the lessons which will save us from sin and death and for everlasting life, if we listen and respond.

As you read the words of Jesus which follow, I ask that you read them with your heart. Let these words speak to your soul as they give light to your mind, and strength to your Spirit.

Listen as you have never listened before; and realize, as you read, that the Message you find in the Sacred Scriptures is true! God does love us and wants our salvation. As St. Paul reminds us in his Letter to the Romans: "Nothing can separate us from the love of God that comes to us through Christ Jesus, Our Lord." Nothing—except our selfishness, our pride, and our sin.

May these Lessons be a bright new chapter in our personal salvation history. May they be the catalyst for our true conversion of heart. May we all accept this invitation to allow God to become the Center of our lives at last. "Seek first His Kingship over you, His way of Holiness. . ." (*Mt.* 6:33).

Fr. Jack Spaulding, Pastor
St. Maria Goretti, Parish
Scottsdale, Arizona
August, 1989

Lessons From Our Lord

SORROWFUL MYSTERIES

SEPTEMBER 20, 1988

My child, I would like you to start being and living the holiness of Me. . .not only in your actions, but in your daily thoughts and feelings. Do not be holy on the surface, be holy within, and throughout your entire body. BE ME!

(Jesus talked to me before each Sorrowful Mystery, beginning with the second mystery).

2ND MYSTERY *(Scourging at the Pillar)*

The pain of My scourging was not the scourge, but in who was doing the scourging. That pain still exists.

I always comforted, but when that time came for the Lord, God, to be comforted, My loved ones could not, because they were afraid. Yes, fear, like in today's world. People live in fear. Where is the trust in the Lord, God's comfort?

3RD MYSTERY *(Crowning of Thorns)*

Then I accepted My thorns for the sake of My people's fear, and forgiveness of their sins, but My people could not accept this. That is the sorrow.

4TH MYSTERY *(Carrying of the Cross)*

Then I carried My cross for My people. But My people will not carry their cross for Me. How weak in faith you are! You all want someone else to carry your cross, and you want eternal life too.

I say to you: "Carry your own cross and carry your brother's and then come into My Kingdom!"

5TH MYSTERY *(The Crucifixion and Death on the Cross)*

My people could not stop at the mockery of Me, but continued with the mockery of My mother, who cried for you at the foot of My cross, and who is still crying for you. She lived My sorrow and is still living it.

Feel the pain she feels.

MERCY

OCTOBER 31, 1988

My child, I shall show mercy on those who have not been merciless! Have mercy on those to whom you wish Me to show mercy.

Do not show any favoritism. Have mercy on all, for all belong to Me.

My people pray for mercy, yet, they do not practice it. Those, who do not know of My Mercy are better off than those who do know it, but will not practice it on their neighbor. Better to be blind and not see, than to see and act blinded!

It is simple...love as you wish to be loved. Treat others as you wish to be treated. If you are not loved or treated fairly, continue on. Your love will be noted by Me.

THE BLESSED SACRAMENT

NOVEMBER 5, 1988

Please come before the Blessed Sacrament...I will speak to you there.

Here, I am present in My Tabernacle, waiting for My people so that I can fill them with My peace. Pay homage to Me, your Lord...I, Who am your source of life!
Do you know what it means to be in front of the Blessed Sacrament?

It is I, Who am here. It is I, Who stands before you! It is I, Who shall grant your heart's desire. It is I, Who awaits, My dear one.
I have been waiting for so long for all to come to Me, so that I can give them true happiness!

EUCHARIST

NOVEMBER 5, 1988
(During Communion)

My dear one, I am now within you. It is in the Eucharist that I am consecrated to you and you to Me.

Many of My people do not realize what it means to receive My Body. My people do not realize the power they receive when they receive the Eucharist.
It is My power...the power of Christ!
I, in you, shall grant your heart's desire. It is I, through Eucharist, Who makes your image one in the likeness of God, because you are receiving My Body. I grant you special graces, not by human desire, but by Mine. You become people of God. All you need do is ask.
My people need to be open to this.

MERCY

NOVEMBER 7, 1988

My dear one, as you have seen, My people are deaf to the words of your Lord. How belittling it is to Me for them to seek help without first asking for the source of their help...the gift of Myself!

People do not listen. They did not listen back in My age and they still do not listen now. They hear what they want to hear. They select their words over Mine.

My impatience with their selection is deepening. Your prayers are comforting My impatience. It is because of My children that I am a generous and patient God. I long to fill My people with so many special gifts, but they will not allow Me, because I am in line in their selection process.

My people will not let Me be their God! They make Me out to be Who they think I should be. How much longer do you think this can continue before man corrupts the gift of this world totally? Man expects to accomplish on his own. The pain I feel is because the beauty of this world was once given as a symbol of the love of God.

Today you gave up a special time with Me, so that you could help My other children. When you comforted My children, you comforted Me.

I would now like to instruct you about My mercy. What is mercy? Who deserves My mercy? Who asks for mercy?

Mercy is the Divine power of My love, which flows out on to whomever seeks it.

One of the many gifts as you receive My Holy Spirit is that of mercy. When you allow My Divine Love to flow from you, out to someone who is in need, that is My mercy flowing out from Me. When you, or any of My children, have mercy on someone, it is equivalent to Me having mercy on that same person...because of My Spirit, which dwells in you.

Mercy is a missing link in loving. You cannot love without being able to have mercy. You cannot have mercy if you do not love! I know this seems very much for you, but you must know the truth.

My people ask for My mercy, but they will not give My mercy, because they select not to love, or they select who they desire to love.

God does not select...neither should His people.

What makes man think he is rich enough that he has the right to love one person and not another? I mean pure love, not sexual love. Man even distorts what love is. A man with 10 shillings is richer than a man with 5, until a man with 20 shillings comes along. That does not mean that the man with 10 shillings has more power to select who he loves than the man with 5 shillings, and the same holds true for the man with 20 shillings.

If you want to have mercy on someone, you need to love that person! If you want mercy in return, you need to allow yourself to be loved!

Mercy, love, Divine power is all possible through all My people, if they would listen and ask for the gifts I wish to pour out on them through My Spirit.

CHRIST ALIVE IN US

NOVEMBER 8, 1988

You see, My child, even today I pray in thanksgiving to My Father for the wonderful gift of the glory My children bring to Me. I prayed for My disciples then, and I pray for My living disciples now...they who are not of this world, but must live in it. I pray for your protection.

It is I, Who am consecrated to you...you and all My children. I live in you, and you live in Me. My Father has granted this gift of glory to Me for all who desire Me.

My disciples live on now, and I am with you, living in My Spirit, as I hold you in My Flesh. This prayer of truth holds for all those believers who seek the truth, the truth of the Living God. The power of God which lives in you, because I am consecrated to you in My Spirit, is for all!

The world cannot accept this, because My people choose, once again, to accept only what they think they can handle. What constraints you put on your own selves.

You, who are given the truth and many gifts, choose not to accept. Let it be as you wish...and when you say to Me:

"Lord, why did you not give these wonderful gifts
and let the truth be known to me?"...I shall say:
"Be gone! You were given abundantly, but chose
not to accept. Now I will select, and you can be
in line for My selection process!"

I want so much to give My people the fresh, pure fruits of life. If My people continue to select the sour fruits, they will wither. My mother, who continues to plead for you, will soon not be allowed. For only My fresh fruits will blossom.

Save! Save! Save the world, child!

For I, the Lord, speak the truth, and am very serious. Have mercy on those to whom you wish Me to give mercy. I shall listen to you, for you listen to Me. Go in peace. My protection and My strength are with you.

SINCERITY

NOVEMBER 9, 1988

My child, we must continue now with the lessons for the children of the world.

Torment of Me in your selection process will result in torment for you in My selection process.

Those, who do their best in loving one another, will not have to stand in line for judgment. I, your Lord, look at the sincerity of your heart. Even when you attempt, but fail, if your attempt to love is sincere, you have not failed.

My dear one, the time of My mercy is at hand. I simply am asking for love, respect and mercy on one another.

Is that too much to request from a God, Who constructed a world of beauty for His people; who were constructed in His likeness and His beauty? You say 'no,' but look around you and observe My people, who say they love. The world was so beautiful, but My people have made it so ugly. There is hope to recapture My beauty. . .but, little time to do so.

I have been telling My people for ages to love, but they have chosen not to do it. Why would they change their hearts now? Their hearts have no beauty.

Did you see that man? He walked in and out of My church. . .and that was his time allotted to Me as a symbol of his thanks. That was his time to share his most intimate thoughts with Me. Tell Me, should I have mercy on him?

RELIGIONS

NOVEMBER 9, 1988

I would now like to talk to you about religions.

People worship in My churches, and claim their form of worship is the most true.

Woe to those who disclaim a form of prayer to My Father.

When the Jews pray to My Father, they pray to Me, for I am One with the Father. The Jews are very much My people. If you were Protestant, would you love Me less? It should be known to all My children that I do not love them less because of the semantics of the dichotomy of religion.

I Am your Lord, God, and I hear all forms of prayer. It is not your form of worship, but your heart that I want. Whether you are Jew or Gentile, you are, because of Me, Who Am!

My people, who analytically debate theological trivia, should be made to know this fact of truth:

I, your Lord, God, love all who come to Me to be loved.

I love in all forms of worship and prayer. It is true that I, through My Body in Eucharist, Am in the purest form of consecration to you. But that is a choice My children have.

Many people will say that because of your religion, you think you are closer to Me. It is not because of your religion, My child, it is because of your open, loving heart.

How do you serve God? By serving His people. Serve by loving one another. Have mercy on one another, so that I will have mercy on you. Be My treasure in heaven by being My treasure on earth. Love will restore My beauty given to this world. How many different ways can I express this message to you? My people want, want, want...but they need to give to receive!

My child, know that I love My people of all religions, but it is through My Blood of the wine, and My Body of the bread, that I live one with you.

RETURN TO GOD

NOVEMBER 10, 1988

Children have been given to My people as a gift! People used to pray for children to My Father, and received them as a sign of His love. To bear a child was a gift...now it is a burden.

My people used to pray for children...now they pray not to have children. They pray, "Oh Lord, do not make me pregnant, or I will have to have an abortion." How carelessly they select their words!

They pray, "Oh Lord, please help me this time, and I will never do it again!" How patient I have been with My children, because of My great love for all. What do they take Me for? I see, and know, the deepest incentives behind your thoughts.

> DO YOU NOT KNOW THAT I AM NOT AT YOUR DISPOSAL, BUT THAT YOU ARE AT MINE?

It touches Me deeply that I must give in order to receive their love. In today's world the people are as wild as they were in My age. They seek external stimuli to achieve inner satisfaction. They rely on synthetic chemicals to make them happy, to make them function. They are relying on these resources for their comfort. I want so much to give them inner strength, but they will not ask.

I want My people to turn back to Me; to pray and to love one another, and to have mercy on one another, so that I will have mercy on them. This is My message:

> I AM A GIVING GOD, BUT WILL NOT GIVE ANY LONGER UNTIL MY PEOPLE RETURN TO ME BY LOVING ONE ANOTHER!

Drugs, sex, abortion, money and power all manipulate My people. There is much evil in the world, because My children have selected this way. What restrictions they place on themselves! If they would turn to Me, there would be no limitations to the geat bounty of gifts I would flourish upon them. This is a truth you must know. You must see the world as I see it. You must pray for them. I have waited a great length of time, and will not wait much longer.

When My people give to the poor, they need to give with their hearts. . .not just when they need to rid their households of clothes or other items. Giving with your heart is not giving when you select to give. Giving with the heart is an openness to helping others, whether it be giving your time, your clothes or your money, but giving with love, and at all times. My people think that giving to the poor is materialistic giving. This is not so.

People who are poor, are not only those in financial need. They are My people who are also poor in Spirit. . .My people who are in need of spiritual healing, so that their hearts can be rich. There are so many of My children who are financially rich, but so poor in Spirit. I wish to make them rich, but they choose not to allow Me to love them, because they think they have everything they need. They restrict their intake of love, but not of power! If people would allow themselves to be loved, then My mercy would flow into them.

Remember, if you want to receive mercy in return, you need to allow yourselves to be loved.

TURN BACK TO GOD

NOVEMBER 11, 1988

My child, I am here now, present in My tabernacle as I have been for so long. Look into My eyes...the eyes of My Heart...My eyes that look into your heart.

My dear one, what do you see? You see people hungry for love. You see what I am seeing. My people hunger for love, but they block receipt of it. I tell you that My people must stop blocking the path of My warmth and intimacy. From My time until this time, My people continue to reject My love, and the time will soon come, when they will no longer have the opportunity to receive My warmth and My intimate Body.

Make no mistake about this! I urge you, My people, to begin to allow My Father, My Spirit, Myself, to dwell in you and fill you with the gift of everlasting life. I will not much longer plead for My people to recognize the truth and turn back to Me, their God.

When I come, it will be during a time of standard, day-to-day functioning. But I tell you...it will be too late to come back! COME BACK TO ME NOW!

If you are in two's, if you are in a group, if you are married, or not, I will only take up those who desire Me now, and not at that point. Yet, to those who respond to this warning, for I speak the truth:

I, your God, trust those who trust in Me.
I, your God, have faith in those who have faith in Me.

The ages have come and passed, but I, your Lord, God, have remained the same. I tell you, My people, take heed of these words:

I shall throw those into the fire of flames, who are not worthy...worthy by their love for one another.

Have mercy, My people! Have mercy on your God by loving one another, so that I, your God, will have mercy on you.

(continuation)

NOVEMBER 12, 1988

There will be many of My people who perish, because they have selected Me last, or not at all! When that time comes, those people will no longer be My people!

I tell you, child, and I will continue to tell you: **I want My people to turn back to Me. . .to live with sincerity, honesty, righteousness and truth. I want My peace to fill their hearts. I have a peaceful Kingdom, and will have only those who seek peace in order to dwell in it.**
It will not be much longer! Make note of this! For the time is short. . .short, My child!

You are tired now, but do not be sad, because the time is near when the good will be weeded from the bad and will return to Me, your living God.
Go in peace! Do not be overwhelmed! I, your Lord, will comfort you.

SIMPLICITY AND TRUST

NOVEMBER 22, 1988

My dear child, how it pleases Me to have My little lambs, My little children, come to Me rejoicing in their God. The purity and openness of their hearts allows Me to fill them with special graces. That is how I wish all My children of all ages would come to Me...with innocence and purity.

My people think that, in order to please Me, they must pray differently than the way My little children pray. You do not have to be extraordinary, and offer sacrifices beyond what you have already been called to do.

My people think they must do so much to please Me. I am only asking for their hearts to be open to My words, so that I can fill them with all the goodness and the grace of joyfulness.

If My people would come back to Me with hearts like children, relying and trusting in Me, with hearts of openness and purity, I would fill them with the freedom and happiness of children. They would be carefree children.

But My people struggle and make things so hard for themselves. If only they would try. **"Just try," say I, Your Lord!**

I, your Lord, am a loving God, Who calls His people to simplicity...simple prayers, simple words of thanks, simple ways. It is in this simpleness that you will be filled with the richness of My treasures. My people do not need to be flamboyant, and worship in a form that would bring attention to themselves. **Pray with your heart...in the quiet of your heart.** My people want power and attention, even in prayer. That is the way of the world now...power!

Know the joy I have when My children come to Me like "little children." It is with hearts of little children that you will gain the treasure of My Kingdom.

FAITH

NOVEMBER 30, 1988

My child, we are now ready for another lesson. . .a lesson about faith. The first step to having faith is surrendering with trust.

Faith is knowing your Lord will bring you out of exile, and living that knowledge with joy, love and happiness, because of the truth.

This is faith: Trusting in Me and My Gospel words. My Gospel is the truth.

You cannot have faith one day, and not the next, because of a change of your mood. This is what many of My people do to Me. One day they trust in Me and have faith that I will care for them. The next day their faith is not so strong, because their feelings are different for that day. Your Lord does not change day to day.

My people may change their feelings day to day, but your Lord does not. I will remain true to My people, as I have said many times in the past.

My people should not mistake faith with their feelings. Faith is trusting in the truth. . .the truth that I shall save them and care for them. It is because of evil that My people struggle, not because of Me! They would rather struggle with their worries and problems, instead of having faith in their God. They must surrender and trust and have faith on a day to day basis not on a time interval of their choice. If only they would try. It is difficult because My people make it difficult.

My words to you have been words I have said in past ages. They are not new, and yet, I am still waiting for My people to try what I am requesting. My child, this is faith. . .a fact not a feeling. . .a grace given to My people. . .a tool of power which is not practiced. Go in peace now. Adieu.

CHARITY

DECEMBER 3, 1988

My dear child, I wish to be glorified in all My children, for they are glorified in Me. It is the prayer that I prayed to My Father for this world, before My Sorrowful Passion ...My wish that all My children would be safe and glorified with Me.

My children have received many gifts from Me. Gifts of love, strength and faith. It is time that you give to each other the gifts that I have given you. **Share your gifts!** They were given to you so that they would be shared with others. Pass on the gift of love, so that those, who are searching, will be brought home to Me.

This is your lesson on charity, the giving of gifts I have given you, for all My people of this world. Charity is a gift; a gift that combines love, faith, trust, joy and hope for others. CHARITY IS THE GIFT OF GIVING YOURSELF.

What a great gift of sharing your love, your faith, your joy, your trust and your hope with others, unconditionally, in My Name. You have been given these gifts to use them. Realize that they have been given to you.

This message is meant for all. Realize the gifts I have given you. Share your gifts, so that you will be given more!

UNITY

DECEMBER 6, 1988

My child, it is through the conception of My Body that you are glorified in Me. It is I, Who make you a priority to Me. It is through love that many lost lambs are found. It is because of My mercy that you have been saved.

LISTEN! IT IS I, WHO AM, WHO MADE YOU!

What do you feel inside? Do you not feel My Body encompassing yours in unity? It is this, My Presence, which you are aware of, which is in all My children. My Body is united in oneness with theirs. Oneness in My Body is a gift, which I have promised to My children. I am present in all My children.

I am present in all My children, as the bond I have promised to them. I came into this world to save you from the evil one, and in forgiveness of your sins, to unite you in oneness to Me.

I wish for My people of this world to know that I am united in oneness with them. I have promised this to My children for their glorification to My Father.

Unity with My Body allows the power of My gifts. . .love, faith and hope. . .to be Me, living them in you!

GIVE YOUR HEART

DECEMBER 9, 1988

My child, the lesson is this: GIVE ME YOUR HEART, AND I WILL GIVE YOU MINE!

By giving Me your heart, you will be trusting. If you trust in Me, you will live in peace and harmony all the hours of your life. I gave My heart to you when I died for you. Give Me your heart, and live in My peace.

Do not despair, do not panic. I have come to save you.

My childen: My love for you is so great!
My Kingdom is yours, should you desire it!
I have given My life for you!
There is nothing I would keep from you. . .
nothing!
You must go now. I am here! I dwell in you!

FASTING

DECEMBER 13, 1988

My dear child, I am here to save. I am here to save you and My people. This is not a game...this is true...for I am Truth, and this is serious.

It is serious because of the many lost souls, who could be turned away from Me because of the lack of tender gentleness, which is needed.

I love My people so. I wish to be with them and make them happy, but they will not invite Me. My people will soon know that you fast for their salvation. It is in fasting that you are made pure.

I fasted for My people. I tell you, they did not care about fasting in My age, nor do they in this present age. When you fast, you are cleansed with My Holiness. The purity of My Spirit dwells in you and cleanses you.

I ask you today to fast in order to purify and cleanse yourself for My mother's coming. I shall purge you and sanctify you in Me. **Blessed are those who fast for their love for Me, and the salvation of others.**

I am not calling you to fast for long periods of time. Simply once or twice a week. Is this asking too much of you? The purest form of fasting is on bread and water, but as you are aware, there are other ways of fasting for those who cannot do the former.

Pray for humbleness and humility. **It is I,** and only I, Who work through you. I am here to save. Rejoice! My peace is with you.

THE BRIDGE

DECEMBER 14, 1988

(Jesus told me to read: *Matthew* 12: 33-42.
John 13: 31-35. *Isiah* 35: 1-10).

I, the Lord, am now here to build a bridge for those whom I have chosen to take My journey, and they will be redeemed.

I shall gather My children of goodness to cross this bridge. No evil will be allowed to cross. Only happiness and peace will come to those who journey with Me.

My little one, I am speaking of a bridge that all My people can cross, if they would allow Me to purify them in My unity. The beauty that blossoms on the other side of this bridge cannot be described. It awaits you, and you will obtain it when you reach the other side.

There are streams and meadows and flowers, which always remain in full bloom, because those who dwell and pass through this pasture are pure of heart, fresh and clean of spirit. Once you are on this bridge, no harm can come to you, because no evil is allowed.

The key to finding the path to this bridge is to center on Me, so that I can purify you and lead you. Happy shall those be, who put their trust in Me, for I shall lead them to the green pastures, which await them across this bridge.

It is My bridge to everlasting life. This bridge shall be destroyed after I have gathered all My children, for no evil shall cross. Go in peace now, My child.

COME TO ME

DECEMBER 15, 1988

> COME, ALL YE WHO ARE HUNGRY, AND EAT
> MY BREAD.
> COME, ALL YE WHO ARE THIRSTY, AND
> DRINK FROM MY WELL.
> COME AND RECEIVE THE JOY AND THE PEACE
> I WISH TO GIVE YOU.

Heed My command, the command to love and drink from My well. **For love is Me,** and if I am at the center of your life, I will unite you with Me in love.

Do not hunger any longer. Come to Me, and I will provide you with bread. It is an invitation to receive My Grace...for all you who desire it shall receive abundantly. There is no pain, no sorrow. It is an invitation to happiness and comfort. I will expiate your sins, and raise you up. I will deliver you to My Father.

> Dwell on Me! Live in Me, and all nations will
> run to you. I will clothe you with garments. I will
> provide as your God has promised. Come to Me!
> I, who have respect for you, wish to unite you to
> Me and exalt you on high in My company.

It is grace I wish to shed on you and all are invited to receive My gift. Come and receive the many treasures which await you!

DIVINITY / FAITH

DECEMBER 19, 1988

It was through My faith in My Father, united with My Blood, that Divine Mercy was shed then, and is shed now. It is faith that is My source of power, and it is faith in Me that is your source of power!

For I am Faith, and I am your source of power!

It is My people who choose to select money, prestige and status as their god, their power. It is in doing this that I am placed last, and not acknowledged as their Divine Power. This, My dear one, is why they will lose their power.

Having faith in Me, and having mercy on one another is acknowledging the unity of My Divinity to My Father. It is with faith that miraculous events happen. The slightest doubt questions My Divinity and is your loss of power!

Make no mistake. . . it is the unfaithful servant that needs signs for acceptance and acknowledgment of My Divinity. It is the faithful servants who are given power abundantly, because they are acknowledging the truth of My Divinity.

It is I Who has faith in you and when you have faith in Me, we are fused together! My mercy flows because of My love and My faith in My Father. It is My Divinity.

That is why I ask that you have faith in Me and mercy on each other; so that you may share in My Divinity.

You either have faith, or you do not!
You cannot have faith one day and not the next!
You cannot have mercy on one another one day and not the next!
There is no middle of the rope. There are only two ends!

I wish for My people to begin practicing faith. Practicing faith is believing in Me, and living in My Divinity.

Now do you understand that it is through faith that you will share in My Divinity, and receive My mercy? It is by grasping this, and by loving, that My mercy flows through you.

I AM FAITH!

IF YOU HAVE FAITH, YOU LIVE IN ME, AND ACKNOWLEDGE MY DIVINITY, WHICH WILL BE SHARED WITH YOU THROUGH MY MERCY.

Go in peace now.

CELEBRATION

DECEMBER 22, 1988

My child, on this, My special day, I take heart in thanking My family, My people, who celebrate in My mother's happiness because the day of My birth was the day of your survival. Fear was extinguished and comfort restored for all those who had faith then, and now, in Me, their Saviour.

The Son of Man came as "Man of Man." (**). **It is I, Who Am, Who still lives as Man of Man, uniting all who desire it, in My Divinity.**

It is not a lesson today, but a proclamation for you and My people. I am here to celebrate the many souls who shall rise and rest with Me. I am here to celebrate with you and in you, in thanksgiving to My Father for the many gifts you shall receive because you have shared your gifts with one another. Those who have shared their gifts shall receive abundantly.

The symbol of Christmas is not only your celebration of My birth. It is My celebration of your renewal. It is a birth that does not come yearly, but daily, for those who seek joy, peace and comfort.

You are My living celebration. This means that you celebrate the good news of My Father daily, which is a festival in its own right. **My child, tell the world that My birth was their salvation! My death, their resurrection!**

(**) The term "Man of Man" signifies Jesus as the Ruler of the human race, giving us a share in His Kingdom.

It is I, Who hope and has faith in all to select the purified good fruits which I offer from My vine. I am celebrating! I will save those who are discouraged, who are suffering, and who are desolate. I celebrate because these, My loved ones, will be renewed on this day of My coming, My birth!

SELFISHNESS

DECEMBER 22, 1988

My child, it is selfishness that keeps My people away from Me. It is their fear of giving up their control that is selfishness.

What is it that My people have by their own control that I, their Lord, would not give them...and more abundantly? They limit their own receipt of gifts. It is even during the celebration of My birth that My people are selfish! Giving gifts is a chore, not a pleasure, and it is those gifts that I have given to My people which are not shared.

Yes, My little one, there are many children who do recognize the truth of sharing My gifts, and who long for more. They shall receive more! Yet, there are those who do not recognize their gifts.

My people need to learn the many facets of My truth! They want to debate the theological commands of My Kingdom, but will not grasp the simple lessons I teach. How can I teach them fully, when they are not willing to learn the basic principles?

Many theologians gather and try to interpret My messages. They cannot accept My words as being exactly as they are written. If I say, "love one another, and have mercy on one another," that is exactly what I mean!

A theologian will take that sentence and read into it various interpretations. This is the problem. They make the Man of Man out to be a distant and complicated God. **The day will come when they will know that I am a God of love and simplicity Who wishes to serve you and your heart's desire.**

RESPECT

DECEMBER 26, 1988

People in your age do not have respect for one another, and so, cannot have respect for me!

This is a continuation of your lesson on selfishness. It is selfishness when My people do not listen; when My people choose to absorb only what they wish; when My people do not respect one another and do not respect Me. How can My people absorb what is to come if they will not allow Me to teach them? They are the people, who do not give respect to their God, but want their God to respect them by acknowledging their wishes. What would you have Me do? Should I fulfill their hearts by granting their wishes to receive their love for the moment?

No, I tell you! I, out of thanksgiving and love for My father, and compassion for My people, will answer their requests, but at the time that is pleasing and is respectful to My Father.

When My people come to Me to pray, I ask that they first pray in thanksgiving to My Father for the many graces He has bestowed upon them, even though they have not recognized them. In a respectful manner, they may then ask Me what it is they wish. I will fill them with what they need.

When My people come to receive My Body at Eucharist, I ask that they fold their hands in prayer, and receive in thanksgiving to My Father for His gift of Me to them. **So many people today come and receive Me in a manner that does not give respect to My Father. This is a selfish habit, and needs to be stopped!**

I wish for My people to understand the many facets of My Kingdom, but they need to understand the basic rules first. It is selfishness which is preventing them from understanding thoroughly. With selfishness there is lack of respect. If you have respect for Me, you would be willing to practice and eat the fruits on the pathway to My Kingdom.

GRATITUDE

DECEMBER 26, 1988

My people have so much for which to be grateful. I have told them that they will share in My Glory and Divinity. If My people would begin realizing their gifts by searching within, instead of searching without, they would live with gratitude and share in My Glory.

It is a gracious and peaceful life if you are grateful for the many gifts you have and notice them in yourself. It is a gratitude which flows over to My Father and it is He Who replenishes you.

There are few people who are grateful today, because they are continuously searching for happiness. I wish to make them happy! If they would give Me their hearts, I would comfort them. It is because of their free will that I will not infringe upon them!

It is I Who respects them, but it is also I Who weeps for them! It is I Who has the treasures of life and wish them to overflow on to you.

It begins with gratitude. . . being grateful, and searching for your inner gifts. My people will never be happy if they continue to search for gifts of momentary pleasure.

I have your gifts of eternal happiness! Simply open your hearts so that you may receive them! By living with gratitude, you shall receive gratitude. I do not mislead My people. It is they, who wish to be misguided by searching for other sources of happiness. This is a lesson for you on gratitude. It is simple. Open your hearts and be grateful! I, your Lord, will overfill you with such happiness, you will never need to search again!

It begins with open hearts to Me, and it never ends. . . in the comforts of My Kingdom's peace and happiness.

GLORY

DECEMBER 29, 1988

The glory of My Kingdom results from the glorification of My Father. All who dwell in My Kingdom are glorified in oneness with My Father. It is glory they receive, who dwell in My Kingdom.

I Am Glory! My Kingdom is Glory! All who dwell in My Kingdom are glorified! That is why you give glory to My Father. . . because I give glory to My Father! **He is Glory! I Am Glory, for I Am One with Him!** You give My Father glory, because I give Him glory, and because I am one with you!

It is through My Blood that we are one with each other. It is a consecration, and it gives glory to My Father. That is why I have said you are glorified in Me and in My Father. It is Our Consecration.

YOU BRING ME GLORY WHEN YOU LIVE MY GOSPEL WORDS.

YOU BRING ME GLORY WHEN YOU LOVE ONE ANOTHER.

YOU BRING ME GLORY WHEN YOU HAVE MERCY.

YOU BRING ME GLORY WHEN YOU ARE FAITHFUL AND OBEDIENT.

YOU BRING ME GLORY THROUGH SIMPLE PRAYERS OF THANKSGIVING.

I, WHO SHARE MY GLORY, BRING YOU GLORY BY GLORIFYING YOU IN ME, AND IN MY FATHER!

KINGDOM

DECEMBER 30, 1988

Glory is thankful worship and praise to My Father. As I have said, giving Me glory is giving My Father glory, and you are glorified in Us.

Let Me tell you something about My Kingdom. If you are glorified in Us, by giving glory to Us, can you not dwell in My Kingdom, which is a Kingdom of Glory, NOW?

My Kingdom consists of life. What I am telling you is that My people seek to dwell in My Kingdom as an after-life. **I am telling you, you can dwell in My Kingdom now by living your life with Me and in Me! I Am life! My Kingdom is life!** If you are glorified in Me, and live in Me now, are you not dwelling in My Kingdom now?

I tell you, there are not many living in My Kingdom now, because they have not heeded My words. My people can live in My Kingdom now. They do not need to wait for an after-life.

If you love one another, heed the commands I have spoken, live in peace and adhere to the principles of My power, I assure, you are living and dwelling in My Kingdom!

You are life! My Father made life, because His Kingdom is life, and He wanted His people to live in His Kingdom. It was His people, My people, who destroyed their life and their living kingdom, the one in which you now dwell.

There are ones who live in Me now, that, I tell you, are living in My Kingdom among those who have destroyed their life and their living kingdom. I am here to save them, to restore their life and to give them the opportunity to dwell in My Kingdom of life.

Make no mistake, those who seek My Kingdom for their after-life need to seek My Kingdom now, and to live in My Kingdom of life now!

For I lived My life in My Father's Kingdom of life, which became your kingdom of life after My death. Dwell in My Kingdom now, with Me, by living in My Kingdom of life.

This is your good news to be shared!
With My Father's blessing, I give you My Peace!

JANUARY 5, 1989

My dear one, I again wish to emphasize the importance of living in My Kingdom now. My Kingdom is your kingdom! And if your life is now united with Mine, you are living NOW in My Kingdom.

It is a choice that all My children have. If you keep yourself pure, and consecrate your life to Me, you will be protected, dwell in My Kingdom, and share in My Glory.

Know that following My way now is not the easiest, because many do not follow My way. As I have told you, I am here to save. **This is the time to bring My children home.**

My dear one, I love you so, because you have allowed Me to love you! When My people love each other, they allow Me to love them! Living in My Kingdom is allowing love to flow like a river from one to another. This lesson is one which should not be taken lightly. That is why I have repeated it, and placed emphasis on it.

PLEASE LOVE ME BY LOVING ONE ANOTHER!
HAVE MERCY ON ME BY HAVING MERCY ON ONE ANOTHER!
LIVE IN ME BY LIVING IN MY KINGDOM NOW!
HELP ME BY HELPING ONE ANOTHER!
REJOICE IN ME, REJOICE WITH ME, REJOICE WITH ONE ANOTHER!
MY FATHER SHALL GLORIFY YOU AS HE HAS GLORIFIED ME!
PLEASE COME!
THE GATES TO MY KINGDOM HAVE BEEN UN-LATCHED!

TRUTH/OPEN HEART

JANUARY 6, 1989

My dear child, as you have seen, when My children truly focus on Me, My Holy Spirit fills them with the knowledge of the truth. The truth is that I give you love, peace, joy, faith and mercy, because I am Love, I am your Peace, I am Joy, I am Faith and I am Mercy.

Why is it so difficult for My people to grasp this truth? It is your salvation, your hope, your strength. If My people would be patient, and calmly open their hearts, and allow Me to fill them with My Spirit, they too would be filled with the knowledge of My truth. I tell you this because it is the first step. . .**allowing Me to love them by opening their hearts.**

What does it mean to "open your heart?"

To open your heart is to allow yourself to love Me by absorbing My goodness. To absorb My goodness is to listen to My Gospel words and live My goodness. It is not difficult, but people struggle because they make it so difficult.

OBEDIENCE

JANUARY 8, 1989

Let us now continue with Friday's lesson on the open heart.

To have an open heart is to accept what I give you gratefully, trusting that I will provide. To have an open heart is NOT placing emphasis and value on YOUR interpretations of what is good or what is bad. It is remaining neutral and open. It is remaining without judgment as much as possible.

All humans judge, but when you make a conscious effort not to judge, you will be open to My goodness.

> This is what entails an open heart:
>
> There are no emotions, because emotions will influence your openness. It is surrendering and remaining neutral to circumstances. It is through this form of obedience that I can fill you completely with My graces and goodness. It is in this form that you will, also, receive and absorb the bonded link of My grace and goodness.
>
> To have an open heart is not to expect according to your desires.

If you expect according to your desires, you block the receipt of the many graces I shed. This is a simple lesson, but one which is so difficult for My people to practice. I tell you this, so that you will learn and be able to receive more. I would not tell you this if I did not love you.

I want all My people to receive and fully share in the glory of My Kingdom. I wish for all to receive My treasures. I am not greedy! I wish to give! I wish to give to you! I wish to give you My treasures, all of them, but you need to open your hearts, so that you will receive them.

Make a conscious effort to remain neutral, to surrender unto Me. **This is obedience.** Remain emotion free, as much as possible, so that I can unite My emotions with yours.

My emotions of goodness will become your emotions. I promise you, as I promise all My children, this fact of My truth.

Please pray now, the chaplet of Divine Mercy to My Father for the salvation of souls, and in thanksgiving for His goodness.

PRESENCE

JANUARY 9, 1989

My people think that because they do not see, do not hear or do not feel My presence, I do not see and do not hear them. This is not true!

I see and hear all! They do not see, because they do not look within. They do not hear, because they do not listen.

I have given them the greatest gift of all...the gift of My Holy Spirit. If they would invite My Spirit to dwell in them, people would see and hear according to what I wish for them to see and hear!

I wish for all My people to forgive one another, be respectful of one another and to remain calm. It is the evil one who stirs up commotion to frighten you, and to make you react by impulse and not by thought!

I listen, My dear people! I do!

It is because I do not answer according to their wishes that they will not practice their gift of faith. They do not realize that their solution may not be the best solution for their intimate happiness.

I, Who only love, fill My people with love and happiness. Those who resist are the ones who struggle. It is they who desire gold, but resist receipt of it, who grasp the iron rod. It is their selection...but my pain!

Please know that I am with you at all times, when invited! Because you think I am not with you, does not mean that I am not. It is when you think that I am not with you that you can be sure that I am.

I see you. I hear you. I love you. Please see Me from within. Listen to My words, and love Me by loving others.

CONTROL

JANUARY 11, 1989

My people blame My Father for many bad events. They cry: "If God loved me, He wouldn't allow this to happen to me."

Why do you think they turn to My Father and accuse Him? It stems from what I have told you before. . .people come to Me only when they need assistance. All other times My children wish to be in control of their lives, instead of allowing me!

They credit good happenings to their effort, and do not give thanks or glory to My Father. When things do not go well for them, they come and plead for help. **I wish to help them, but, because they wish to control, I cannot reach their hearts.** If people would only surrender to Me, and give Me their problems by giving Me their hearts!

It is because they do not surrender, or fear losing their control, that I cannot offer them to My Father. When the outcome is one which is not in accordance with their expectations, they blame My Father. **It is the evil one they should blame!**

It is he who takes joy in filling them with pain, and it is My people who allow him to do this!

My people need to surrender their control to Me. I will then be able to fill them with My radiance. This also is part of obedience. **The most difficult thing for My people to do is to give to Me their control!** They are afraid they will lose their power. How can I express the seriousness of this lesson on control?

By trying to hold on to power, they will lose it, because they are grasping the wrong source of power. BY SURRENDERING YOUR CONTROL, YOU SHALL GAIN IT, BECAUSE YOU SHALL BE GAINING MY CONTROL! Being afraid of following My ways because of the need to surrender control, is an emotion placed in you by the evil one!

This is because he has fear that, if you surrender control to Me, he would lose his control over you. There is no justice in fear, because I am not fear!

So trust in Me when I say to surrender unto Me with an

open heart. You will gain control...MY CONTROL...and you shall never fear again. You will only be filled with My goodness, My happiness, My mercy, My power, My love and My peace!

USE OF TIME

3:00 P.M. (same day)

My dear one, it is necessary for you to take two lessons today, because time is short.

Not only are My people afraid to surrender to Me, because of the fear of losing control, they are not willing to allow Me to help them or comfort them. It is a timetable. When My people feel like giving glory to My Father, they do, but on their own allotted days.

Sundays should not be the only time allowed for prayer. Sunday was the last day created, given to you as a day of rest. My people pray on their own timetable and at their desire.

I tell you that prayer is ongoing! Not only when you feel like praying should you take the time. Work is a form of prayer! Pleasure is a form of prayer, united with purity of heart. You see, My people have programmed the world of time, and they have used their time wastefully. Prayer is scheduled last or not at all for many of My children's timetable.

I am telling you that time is now running out! This was not of My will! It has been of My people's will! You who were given freedom and beauty have bound your freedom with your law. You who are narrow minded, not open to beauty and so analytical, have destroyed your beauty because you have spent so much "time" analyzing and debating, instead of accepting and embracing your gifts.

It is because you have devised a restricted timetable, which has put My Father last, that your time is now ending. You created your ugliness, and it is you who wish to dwell in it.

Do not blame My Father for a disaster created by yourselves. Use your time wisely. **Put Him first, and you shall be first.** Reconstruct the beauty of your world. I tell you,

you cannot survive without My Father.

He, Who is patient and a God of Love, will destroy those who destroy His beauty and His love.

> Amen, Amen, I say to you, Heed this command!
> Beware! Put My Father first in prayer, in love.
> Change your agenda to one which glorifies My
> Father or you shall be destroyed.
> Love one another.
> Receive the many beauty-filled graces by opening
> your heart and living in thanksgiving!

My dear one, I am sorry that you have had to be subjected to these words. I, Who am in pain, tell you that I live your pain! I wish for My loved ones to be joy-filled. As they deny Me, they deny My Father and His love. He will not allow His love and beauty to be destroyed.

It is My hope that My people heed My words, for My Father has now constructed His own timetable! Go in peace.

PRAYER

7:30 P.M. (same day)

My dear child, please allow Me to explain to you this last lesson. It was not to frighten you. You see, My people pray when they wish to and at the designated times of their own selection. I am saying that prayer is not only for Sundays. Prayer is an offering, and everything you do should be in a form of prayer and thanksgiving.

If you offer your work as a form of prayer, you will be glorified, because My Father will be glorified. If you offer your lovemaking as a form of prayer, your marriage will be united in a deeper pure love. You see, whatever you do, whatever you say, whatever you think, should be offered as a prayer —one of thanksgiving.

My people have set an agenda of their own time allotment, and so they regulate the many graces they receive. They separate prayer from pleasure, from work, and from love. I care for My people. I love My people and I wish for them to be happy. **I tell you, My people cannot continue as they have in the past.**

Pray, not only in a church on selected days. Pray at all times in everything you do. Pass on your love, your respect, and your mercy to one another. . .offering it as a form of prayer. Do not select a time for prayer and a time for work. Work is a form of prayer and a gift.

Allow the love of prayer to flow through you, and in you, in all things. This will restore the beauty needed, once again, originally given and created by My Father.

This is not meant to frighten you. You must know the truth. My Father has constructed a timetable.

There is no need to fear! There is a need to change!

JESUS' LOVE

JANUARY 12, 1989

If you cry because of your love of Me, imagine how much I cry because of My love for My children. I love them so much that you cannot understand that level of love.

I tell you, My heart aches with much pain for My people because of the great love I have for them. My people have the desire for love, but not the willingness to love, so they are controlled by demons of fear, disappointment, hopelessness and worry.

If only they would be willing to allow Me to help them! If only they would be willing! They are strapped in by "control."

They are so convinced that they can control their lives better than I could. Then, when their fear of survival has weakened them, they cry out to My Father, and damn Him for turmoil that could have been prevented had they allowed Us to control their weakness.

I tell you, My pain comes from wanting to help My people, but they will not allow Me. Please believe Me when

I say: "It is not I Who bring your turmoil."

If you believe Me, you believe in Me, and you believe in My Father's goodness, which is My Divinity.

How can I express to you the seriousness of this truth and the longing I have to fill My people with love and happiness? How much would I give to My people, if they would allow Me!

My child, to the depths of the principalities of My power I would give to them, and desire to now!

This is not a game. This is real! My people think that because they do not see, it is not real. **I am alive, and dwell among you!**

Your theologians will attempt to decipher this meaning, I assure you. They, instead, should pray for the discernment of My meaning in their lives.

My dear one, what I see and what I hear grieves Me, because of My love for My people. My weariness stems from the pain which My mother feels when she comforts and is not comforted in return!

I have been explaining this to you, so that you understand the truth of what is to come if My people do not change and commence giving glory to My Father.

GIFTS

JANUARY 12, 1989

My child, I wish to teach you about gifts.

I do not limit the number of graces and gifts given to you. It is you who limit the number of gifts, by limiting your receipt of them. One gift may be more profound to you than another, but I do not limit how much I give to you.

At this point, there are very few receiving My gifts and there are few wishing to dwell in My Kingdom. I have not stopped giving My gifts. They have not accepted them, because of the hardness of their hearts. One gift is not better than another. All My gifts reflect the gifts of My Father!

From the perception of My people, one gift may seem to be more powerful, but I assure you, all gifts have the same powerful impact. When I ask you to share your gifts with one another, this awakens you to become aware and open to receive many more graces.

PLEASE DO NOT PLACE SUPERIORITY OR GREATER IMPORTANCE ON ONE GIFT OVER ANOTHER! PLEASE DO NOT! My Father's gifts are all of the same beauty and value in magnitude and importance. Do not exemplify envy for others! My people do this so frequently. They are not happy with the gifts they have and envy others, wishing for their gifts.

I assure, if you wish to receive selected gifts, show Me your desire to receive them by loving one another, not by being envious! Being envious will only harden your heart beyond extremes!

Be grateful for the gifts you have. Receive more by asking, accepting, and having faith in Me. The stronger your faith, the more you will be aware of the gifts given, and the more you will have the desire to receive.

To have faith is to trust. Remember, the least questionable doubt weakens your unity with Me in My power.

MERCY

JANUARY 12, 1989

I wish to tell you how My people destroy their gifts by destroying one another! My people live in anger, in bitterness and in fear. My people take matters into their own hands as a way to seek revenge on one another. They think this will gain them power.

I, your Lord, tell My people to have mercy on Me by having mercy on one another. . .and My people do not listen! They show their love for Me by seeking revenge on one another. They show their love for Me with anger and rage. This is not mercy! What is "Mercy?"

Mercy is love, is forgiveness. It is My goodness, which flows out as a Divine blessing. It is not having pity. It is showing pity by loving and forgiving to the deepest level of My people's souls.

When you have mercy on one another, you share in My glory and My Divinity by dwelling in My Kingdom. My Divinity is goodness.

If I do not hesitate to give you all that I have, would I not share My Divinity with you? I tell you:

My Kingdom, and all I have, is yours! There is nothing I would not give to you!

I gave My life for you, so that you could have life. Now, I tell you, that I give My Kingdom, My Glory and My Divinity to those who seek it!

You know that to dwell in My Kingdom and to share in My Divinity and goodness, you must share My love by having mercy. There are so many of My people who need My mercy. I am now here to shed My mercy!

My child, people will say to you that this is a personal matter between you and your God. **I tell you, this is not a personal matter! This is for My people of this world.** I wish to save them, and to invite them to live one with me in My Kingdom. They must begin to love and to have mercy on one another. My people must not take lightly these words, for My Father will not take lightly the consequences to come for not adhering to His Command!

Return and restore the beauty of one another by loving and having mercy. Stop your killings. Stop, I tell you, and love! You are destroying the goodness of My Father's Kingdom, which He gave to you! Fight the evil one! Do not join his side! Fight him with prayers and love! Please, hear My plea!

Your world is being destroyed, and it is you who are destroying it through hatred and indifference. Return to good and pure ways. Begin by having mercy on one another. Begin loving. Begin having respect. Begin treating one another with dignity. BEGIN!

The day will come when the people, who do not believe these words, will know that what I have spoken is true, and it will be their sorrow. . .for it will be too late!

My child, I, your Lord, love My people. I wish for My people to restore peace by living in peace.

JANUARY 17, 1989

(Jesus taught me to pray the "Jesus Rosary" differently, and asked me to pray specifically for certain intentions).

THE AGONY IN THE GARDEN:
Intention: Prayers for peace.
Five "Our Father's" then, "Jesus, be our protection and strength."
Hymn...say: "Glory, glory, glory, alleluia! It is today we are consecrated in you."

SCOURGING AT THE PILLAR:
Intention: Conversion of sinners.
Same prayers.

CROWNING WITH THORNS:
Intention: Cancer patients and the innocent victims of AIDS... (men, women and especially children, at birth, from transfusions, etc.)
Same prayers.

JESUS CARRIES HIS CROSS:
Intention: The unemployed, the poor, desolate, homeless.
Same prayers.

THE CRUCIFIXION, JESUS DIES:
Intention: Those disabled and retarded, who are pure of heart.
Same prayers.

THE RESURRECTION:
Intention: Priests, their celibacy, and devotion to Our Lord.
Same prayers.

THE ASCENSION:
Intention: Abortion!...first bead for the women, second bead for the aborted children, third bead for forgiveness for the destruction of the gift of life.
Same prayers.

HOLY SPIRIT:
Intention: The souls in Purgatory!
The first six beads are "Glory be to the Father, etc." and the last bead is "Glory Be" specifically for the most forgotten soul.

COMPASSION

JANUARY 18, 1989

Compassion is the purity of loving, to the point at which idiosyncrasies have no meaning. It is to love someone beyond their human weaknesses and mistakes. To have compassion, you must see Me, your Lord, beyond any obstacle. To have compassion is to see Me in every person. Compassion is a form of mercy. . .for to have mercy on My children is to have compassion for them!

Do you understand that compassion envelops love to a point where mercy flows? I healed through My Compassion. . .passion for My God, co-existing with the unity of My brothers. All, who belong to My Father, are brothers to Me. . .**brothers, meaning fellowship in the male and female gender!**

This is compassion: Having a passion for your brothers, regardless of their insecurities and faults, because I dwell in them. It is a form of love, mercy and respect. It is a pure passion. It is not feeling sorrowful for someone. It is sincerely seeing the purity of My Passion co-existing in unity with their love.

That is why I tell you to see Me beyond your brother's noticeable faults. I healed because I saw My Father's Passion beyond My brother's sinfulness! I had compassion for them because I had passion for My Father, which I saw dwelling in them, co-existing in His Unity!

You must do the same. You must always see the good in My people, not the bad. When someone is angry, look beyond their anger and see me in their beauty. When someone is spiteful, look beyond their spitefulness and see their desperation for love! Have compassion for them because, when you have compassion for My people, you are having compassion for Me, a passion co-existing in the Unity of oneness with My Father.

All My people are sinful and **it is only I** Who can purge them and offer them to My Father!

REFLECTION

JANUARY 19, 1989

My people continue to analyze all good things. They cannot accept something good as being delivered by My Father. They do not believe that anything like a Divine Power could be possible; THERE MUST BE AN EXPLANATION FOR EVERYTHING!

Then there are the people who destroy the beauty sent by My Father. They blame My Father and shout in exclamation that He did not save them. It is your law. You question and hesitate to believe the truth, and are quick to pass judgment on My Father as the One Who allows destruction. It is My people who allow destruction. It is because they have invited demons of hatred and revenge to manipulate and deplete their source of goodness and love.

Child, I, your Lord, am so very weary of repeating and pleading to My people for their love. You are wasting this holy land, and My Father shall soon take action! You, who were created in the likeness and image of Me, are not walking in My likeness or image!

I, your Lord, never sought revenge.
I, your Lord, never hated.
I, your Lord, only saw beauty and love in My brothers.
I died for you as an offering for your sins.
I gave My life so that you could have life.
My people are destroying their lives.
I, your Lord, tell you that I am weary of pleading for your salvation.

If it is your wish to destroy the gift of beauty and life, given out of the purity of My Father, so be it! It is your choice!

Do not say you were not given the opportunity to choose! It is your free will. However, you are destroying your own freedom. So be it!

This is all I shall say to you today. . .this is all. All that was given to My people is being taken away, because of the destructive hands and hearts of My people.

TRINITY

JANUARY 23, 1989

I would like now to define for you the meaning of the revelation of the Most Holy Trinity. . .the Father, the Son and the Holy Spirit.

It has always been a mystery to My people. The Trinity is three distinct Persons: My Father, My Spirit, and I, Who live together in Unity as One Body.

The symbol of the Trinity is a triangle. That symbolizes the flow from the Father to the Son and to the Holy Spirit, back to the Father or to the Son, remaining as One Body.

When I say you live one with Me, one with My Father and one in My Spirit, I say it is the Blessed Trinity that dwells in oneness with you! It is the symbol which is given to all My people and it is the mark within and throughout the body of My people. It really is no mystery!

My people visualize this as a mystery because the Trinity represents the Father, the Son and the Holy Spirit as One, yet in three separate distinct Persons.

As I have said to you, I live in My people, My Father and My Spirit live in My people in oneness with Me! Is that not the Blessed Trinity living in them? Cannot My people live in oneness with the Trinity?

It is the scope of the universe that Our people are invited to live one with Us in the Blessed Trinity.

THE DEFINITION OF THE TRINITY IS THE FATHER, IS THE SON, IS THE HOLY SPIRIT UNIFIED AS ONE BODY, LIVING IN THREE DISTINCT PERSONS. IT IS ALSO THE SEAL OF MY PEOPLE LIVING IN UNITY AND ONENESS WITH US.

The Church has a difficult time understanding how one can live in oneness and unity with the Trinity. I tell you that through love, all My people are living in oneness with each other, and are united to the Most Holy Trinity in Our Oneness!

Love is your key to unified oneness. Love is your revelation. . .to understanding the truth of being unified in oneness in the Trinity. Love flows from the Father to the Son and to the Spirit, and it is through love that We flow on to you!

It is through love that you unite to Us and flow with Us in Our Oneness. This is how you are made one in each other. . .through the Blessed Trinity, where you are one with Us.

It is through love that it is all possible. . .LOVE!!

ENVY

JANUARY 24, 1989

I would like all My people to know of My great love for them, but even when they hear of this love, they live in envy. I wish for my people to come to Me.

It is because of My great love for them that I am using this instrument to teach them and make known My love for them in this age!

All of My people are blessed when they come to Me with open hearts. There is no one more blessed than another! Instead of My people opening their hearts to Me, they become envious of one another.

> Envy closes My people's hearts! It is envy which destroys your life. It is Love which gives you life. I, your Lord, am Life, for I am Love! Focus on Me. Center your life on Me, and envy will be destroyed!

The good and the bad cannot live together! It is like oil in water. . .it separates. The bad shall be separated from the good.

Those who center on Me shall be purified and shall be separated from those who chose to be without their God. It is the same principle with envy.

Envy is bad, My child. When you focus on Me, envy is destroyed, because nothing bad is able to survive with the purity of good! I am Pure. I will purify My people.

When My people are envious, they do not allow Me to shed My love into their hearts in order to destroy their envy, because their hearts are closed!

On the contrary, if they will allow Me to be at the center of their lives, any irritation, like envy, will only be short-lived. It cannot survive in the goodness of My Divinity and Kingdom.

This is truth! You can be irritated by badness and envy, but it is sure not to survive in My Love!

It is envy, My child, that closed My people's hearts in My age. It was envy that made them stray from being compassionate, which made them merciless people. It is the same today.

Do not seek envy. . .open your hearts!
Seek My love, which is overflowing abundantly for you.
Seek compassion, My compassion.
Be merciful people.

I tell you to go upstream when you are all going downstream! Change the current; allow envy to flow out of your lives, and love to flow into your lives.

Seeking power, money and prestige as your god is centering on envy! Seek love and compassion, and gain power by destroying envy!

JEALOUSY

JANUARY 26, 1989

Today I would like to teach you the difference between envy and jealousy. JEALOUSY IS PURE HATRED FOR ONE ANOTHER!

Envy is the path towards jealousy, which hardens your heart. When you have envy, you close your heart. It is like an iron gateway to a dungeon that closes little by little!

As My people continue to be envious, their hearts harden and close little by little, until they are closed...shut tight...like a drawbridge gate! That is why I say to you that envy only hardens your heart.

With jealousy, your heart is already closed, and there is hatred! Envy will lead you to be merciless people, because your hearts harden. If you center on Me, your envy will not turn into jealousy, because it will not be able to survive.

Love supersedes all...I am Love! If you focus on Me, you will be filled with Love, and your envy will be destroyed.

Now you understand the difference between envy and jealousy. It is envy which is the destructive poison. It leads to hardened hearts, jealousy and a merciless people.

THE NEARNESS OF GOD

JANUARY 27, 1989

My child, so many of My people want to help in My mother's plan. They do not realize that they are already helping in her plan!

My people are waiting for something out of the ordinary to happen. They do not realize all that they have done, or are currently doing, that is helping My mother, and is glorifying Me.

You see, My mother's plan is so very simple. This world is accustomed to extravagant galas! This gala is very simple, and shall be the most beautiful of all!

My people continually say, "When is it all to happen?" They are waiting for an event which they have structured in their minds. They do not realize that it IS happening, and it is happening now!

Do not prepare as if you have time to spare, at your desire, or on your timetable. Prepare and live as if today were the day you would be christened a knight. Be on your best behavior! Have sophistication, and respect one another. Prepare by living each day with your best effort. Be loving and be at peace.

My people always try to outdo their brothers. It is only in love, simplicity and peace that you will be brought My comfort!

My people think that apparitions are the gala to come. They have no conception of the breadth or depth of My mother's plan. That is because My people are narrow-minded, and have predetermined the organization of My mother's gala.

I wish for My people to know that their God is tangible! They pray to Me as if I am so distant. This is because they place Me at a distance. I am a peaceful, loving Man, Who came into your world as Man of Man, because of My Father's love for His people. I suffered, I cried, I laughed...as you...so that you could share in My Glorification...so that YOU COULD HAVE ALL THAT I HAVE!

My people have allowed themselves to think that God lives in a far-away place. They, through their imagination, have distorted My Father's Kingdom as being one which is not attainable. Do not belittle yourselves! I, your Lord, am tangible!

It is like having a loved one go away for awhile. Do you not feel the love and presence of your loved one, even though you do not see him? It should be the same in your love for Me.

Do not place Me at a distance. I tell you, I am as close to your heart as you will allow Me! I wish to dwell in you and you in Me. My people need to allow Me!

This plan, My mother's gala, is so simple that My people will be confused, because of the lack of complication or extravagance. It is so simple and beautiful that My people will desire to live in My simplicity and the beauty of love. There will no longer be panic. . .only peace!

Panic, confusion, hatred, envy, fear, revenge, disrespect, pain and suffering will no longer exist, because evil will be destroyed!

COME ONE, COME ALL, ENDURE NOW! LIVE IN PEACE AND LOVE. LIVE WITH ME IN MY KINGDOM!

PRAYER OF THE HEART

JANUARY 30, 1989

My child, I do not wish for My people to pay homage by their lips, but to pay Me homage with their hearts. **I do not want their words, I want their hearts**.

It is one thing to give Me praise by speaking words from your lips, but it is true glory you give Me when you give Me praise with your heart!

Many of My people come before Me and speak the words of prayer to My Father out of habit. It is a lip service! I wish for My people to digest the words they pray to My Father, with their hearts. This is the form of prayer which glorifies Him, My Spirit, and Me, Who is One in Them.

It is like telling someone you love them with your lips, but not meaning it with your heart! There is no need to say a list of prayers to glorify My Father. It is better to sit quietly and absorb His Presence, to say, "I love You," and mean it with your whole heart...than to say, out of repetition and habit, a list of prayers!

How much glory you bring to Him, when you recite your prayers with your heart and not your lips. I assure you of the glory which is given to My Father, when you say, "I love You," and simply sit in the company of His Holy Spirit!

It is equivalent to sitting in the presence of a loved one without having to exchange words, because of the recognizable love established. There is so much comfort in this form of prayer.

It is also comparable to a mother sitting with her child, comforting her child with her presence. It is the same that I wish of My people. I wish for them to allow Me to be in their presence and comfort them. I wish for them to begin praying with their hearts and not their lips. I wish for them to comfort Me by simply sitting quietly and absorbing the awareness of My presence.

This will glorify them in Me. This will glorify them in My Father, Who is One with Me.

MY PEOPLE, I, YOUR LORD, ASK FOR YOUR HEARTS SO THAT I CAN GIVE YOU MY HEART AND GLORIFY YOU IN THE ONENESS OF MY FATHER.

ALLOW ME TO CONSECRATE MY HEART TO YOURS.

ALLOW ME, PLEASE, MY PEOPLE, TO LOVE YOU.

I WISH TO GIVE YOU MY KINGDOM.

I WISH TO SHARE MY DIVINITY WITH YOU.

ALLOW ME, MY PEOPLE.

PLEASE, ALLOW ME BY GIVING ME YOUR HEARTS!

ALLOW JESUS' LOVE

FEBRUARY 1, 1989

My dear one, your world has so many troubles because of the hatred which exists.

So many of My people rely on medications in order to have control of their lives, in order for them to function. They rely on medications, instead of Me, for control. They cannot function without their medicine, their "source for relief" in which they place their entire trust and confidence.

I, their Lord, am placed last, or not even placed, in their lives. They would rather put their trust in synthetic chemicals as their source of comfort, instead of their Lord.

It is hatred, power, prestige, and the stress of these factors, that have resulted in the corruption of this world. If only My people would allow Me to love them! They do not, My child, they do not!

If My people allowed Me to love them, they would be loving one another, because I would fill them with such peace and love that this would be the only transmission possible unto each other.

This, as I have told you before, is the first step. . .allowing Me to love you by opening your hearts. My people will not even try! My people will not even gather as a community and pray together. They say there is no need to go to church, because they can accomplish the same "love" for one another without going to church. But they love according to a definition of their own law.

So My people continue to compete with each other to survive. This leads to spitefulness and envy, which leads to jealousy and hatred, which leads to revenge.

All of this leads to depression, anxiety and feelings of hopelessness, which leads My people to rely on synthetic chemicals as a source of comfort and control of their lives!

My people make things so complicated. If they would center on Me, there would not be hatred. There would not be anxiety. There would not be depression. There would not be any of the things of which I have spoken, because I AM LOVE, I AM PURE AND I AM GOOD.

If you centered on Me and allowed Me to love you, you would be filled with love, purity and goodness. You would be filled with life! It is simple!

There is only one step My people need to take, and this is to allow Me to love them by opening their hearts. It is when one opens his or her heart and another does not, that there is conflict!

HOWEVER, I, YOUR LORD, ASSURE YOU, IT IS THE ONE WHOSE HEART IS OPEN AND FILLED WITH LOVE WHO WILL SURVIVE BY DESTROYING THE HATRED IN THE OTHER!

Destroying hatred by loving is gaining life now. . .Eternal Life! Attempting to destroy love by hating is sure to destroy your life. People who are resentful and power-filled from destroying the goodness of another, by attacking their inner feelings, will only be destroying their own lives.

My child, it is so very important that My people know of this message. They are destroying their lives by destroying the inner core of each other's hearts through hatred. . .and reciprocating with hatred instead of love!

If they would begin to love, they would destroy the hatred, because they would be allowing Me to love them!

SEEK ME, DESIRE ME!

FEBRUARY 3, 1989

My dear one, My lesson to you and My people is this: I, YOUR LORD, DWELL IN ALL WHO INVITE ME TO DWELL IN THEM.

It is through the power and strength of your faith, and your persistence in loving, that allows you to walk with Me, talk to Me and touch Me!

My people need to grasp on to their faith and know that I dwell in them. They seek the blest in hopes that they will be brought to holiness and to Me. This is wrong! They need to seek Me in themselves and then they will grow in My holiness! **It will be I,** Who brings them to My Father! They need to accept Me! I will make them holy and blessed!

The shy, the weak, the downtrodden need not turn away in sorrow, thinking I have not noticed them. I do notice them. I hear them. I have taken them to My Heart!

Rejoice! Hold on in the strength of your faith and know that I, your Lord, live in holiness in all who desire Me... ALL...not some...ALL! I give My Holiness...not to some...but to all, who desire!

So, fear not, those of you who fear you are not remembered or noticed! I came to this world to take you, personally, into My Kingdom! **It is I, your Lord, Who loves you! It is I, your Lord, Who asks you to love Me by loving one another.**

Please be strong in your faith. It is your power which unites you in oneness with ME. SEEK ME AND DESIRE TO GROW IN MY HOLINESS!

Seek Me. I shall fill the gap in your love!

Love one another and you shall be loved in return. It is possible for all to attain the Kingdom, where I invite you to dwell in holiness. It is all possible...through love!

SERVICE

FEBRUARY 5, 1989

I wish for My people to walk with Me and to touch Me by touching others with their love!
When you love someone, you love Me.
When you feed someone, you are feeding Me.
When you clothe someone, you are clothing Me.

You have heard this before, but they are not just words. I tell you this is true, for I live in all. DO FOR ME BY DOING FOR OTHERS. Please believe your Lord!

I tell you that all your work does not go unnoticed. There is not one of My people I do not notice when they love, feed and clothe My poor ones...not one! **I notice all, for they have loved Me, clothed Me and fed Me.**

There is also not one of My people I do not notice, who hates, steals and kills My dear ones. **I notice, for they hate Me, steal from Me and crucify Me!**

I have told you that if you desire Me with all your heart and wish to serve Me, you must serve My people, for I am here to serve My people. If you wish to reign with Me in the oneness of My Trinity, your heart must be one with Mine. And if you are one with Me, your wish will be My wish, which is to serve My people!

This can all be possible when My people allow Me into their hearts. As My Heart is united to yours, your only desire to serve Me becomes My desire, which is to serve My people; to bring them to My Father, to love them, to feed them My body and blood, to clothe them with My clothes, to offer them My Divinity, My goodness, and to invite them to dwell in My Kingdom!

This is not the way today. Today, people who ask for money for food...people really in need...are told, "I work hard for my money; go find another source to aid you; go get a job!" They do not share, or attempt to help My needy ones.

My people do not realize that what they have...I have given them! IN THEIR GREEDINESS, THEY DO NOT REALIZE THAT I CAN ALSO TAKE AWAY! IT IS MY MOTHER WHO IS SO LOVING, WHO CALMS MY ANGER AND COMFORTS MY SORROW!

These lessons are to be made known to My people of this world, for they are their lessons.

Hold on to Me and your unending power of faith in My Trinity. It is the time of My Divine Mercy! It is the time to save. I am here to save.

All who desire to live in My Unity, My Kingdom, take heed...hear My Words! All who do not, let it be your choice, and dwell with the evil one in his flames of unending pain!

> IT IS YOUR CHOICE. THERE IS NO TURNING BACK...AMEN, AMEN!
> BLESSED BE THE MOST GLORIOUS ONE ON HIGH.
> BLESSED BE HIS HOLY NAME AND BLESSED BE HIS HOLY PEOPLE, WHO GAVE HIM GLORY AND DWELL IN HIS KINGDOM...AMEN, AMEN.

(Lent follows and a time of forty days during which no message of any kind is received from Our Lord or Our Lady.)

DIVINE MERCY

APRIL 2, 1989

On this, the Feast of My Divine Mercy, I shed My mercy and forgiveness on My people. To those who wish forgiveness, it shall be granted.

My Mother prays for My loved ones, that they may be worthy of My promises. It shall be granted. She is My Queen of Mercy! Please take note of these words on this so-very-special feast.

My dear people, it is today, the Feast of My Divine Mercy, I invite you to celebrate and be guests at My table! It is today, My mercy and the mercy of My Father has been shed upon you. Forgiveness and love are upon you.

Celebrate, My people. Rejoice in your merciful God. I have love, goodness and many gifts of grace to bestow upon you.

For all who ask for forgiveness, mercy and everlasting life on this day, shall receive it ever so abundantly.

COME, MY DOORS ARE OPEN. Eat My food and drink plentifully from the grapes of My vine at My feast. It is a joyous occasion, and I wish all to be honored guests!

No one shall go thirsty or hungry. My feast is NOW and you are welcomed, forgiven and ever-so-much loved! Receive My gifts, for it is today that I shall give and you shall receive ever so graciously!

My people of this world, join together. For it is today that you are united to Me:

> To My world of peace; My world of love;
> My world of hope, compassion, joy, charity, strength, faith and truth;
> My world of eternal happiness;
> To My people of God; My people of faith, faith in My Power;
> My everlasting life in My Kingdom!
> Go in peace and celebrate. My Father's Mercy is being shed!

To any and all of My children in need of Divine Assistance from Me, with this prayer I shall not deny any request, for it is My Divine Mercy and Compassion which shall save!

PRAYER OF DIVINE MERCY

O Heavenly Father, O God of Beauty, of Love, I give you my heart. I surrender unto You my life. I abandon to You my soul. Pour forth Your Divine Spirit of Mercy, and shed Your love on me by creating Your beauty in me.

Master of Mercy, have mercy on me, a poor sinner.

Allow me to sing hymns of praise with the Cherubim and Seraphim of Angels in Your Kingdom of everlasting beauty, everlasting peace.

Do not deny me Your Mercy, for I give You my heart this day. Unite my heart to Yours and protect me in Your cloak of purity.

Today is a new beginning in which I have mercy on You, my God, by having mercy on myself and others!

Grant me the favor of your everlasting peace.

Have mercy on me this day and for eternity. . .Amen, Amen!

HUMILITY

APRIL, 8, 1989

My dear one, I wish to teach you now about humility.

Humility can only be given after the heart has been opened. I cannot give the gift of humility unless the heart is open and willing to accept, for humility is accepting all that is given graciously and with unconditional love. It is helping others and giving of yourself.

Humility is allowing Me to grant you everlasting life through the gift of others. It is accepting ALL of which I give to you. To receive My gifts, it is necessary to have an open heart.

Humility is a great gift, because humility is giving unto Me totally. **It is I Who give unto you My whole being totally.**

This is humility—accepting with unconditional love all which I bring to you through your opened heart! It is giving Me your whole being totally by giving yourself to others in need of My love and mercy. That is why it is such a gift. By helping others in need of My love and My mercy, you are sharing in My love and in My mercy.

Humility is a gift which shall be granted to all who come to me with an open heart and request to live in My love and in My mercy. Humility, the mercy of unconditional love.

PRIDE

APRIL 9, 1989

Let us now continue.

I gave you a lesson on humility, one which is so important but usually one of the last to be accepted by My people. That is because of My people's pride and pride is always last in being offered up to Me. My people want to be gods themselves and rulers of their lives. It is because of this that there are so many destructions of kingdoms—man-made kingdoms.

My Kingdom is the only kingdom that no destruction comes to or creates. I tell you that pride is a kingdom that My people create and destruction comes to the kingdoms of pride because of the ego! If My people would put their pride in Me, their Lord, there would be no destruction! To do this you need humbleness and humility, which you cannot receive without giving Me your heart.

So you see, My dear one, all My lessons stem from first giving Me your heart and then receiving the oh-so-many fruitful gifts of grace.

I assure you this lesson on pride will be one that many shall not grasp or choose not to grasp. That is because accepting this lesson and offering to Me your pride will conflict with the kingdom of pride they have created within themselves—their kingdom of "I am god and only I can rule."

The reason for the wars you create is because of your pride in yourselves, instead of pride in Me, your only God.

This is the end of the lesson on pride. Go now in peace, **for I am peace.**

FEAR

APRIL 16, 1989

My dear one, do you know why so many of My people are afraid of Me? They are afraid because they fear I will ask something of them. They are afraid they will have to give up their control of their lives! Many are so comfortable in their lives that they fear I would lead them into another direction.

If I were at the center of their lives, they would not need to fear. If I were at the core of their souls, there would be no need for change! The only direction they would be led, would be onto My path of light, My bridge. Then they would truly lead comfortable lives! It is better to allow Me to direct their lives to My Father's Light now than at a time more convenient for them. It is not a painful path!

> BETTER TO ALLOW ME TO GUIDE YOU TO MY
> BRIDGE THAN TO FIND THE PATH TOO LATE
> WHEN MY GATES HAVE CLOSED!

My journey is one which brings you eternal, life-long happiness. Perhaps My people do not know the meaning of eternal. It you want eternal happiness, you need to make the effort and allow Me to direct and guide you, resting in My peace.

Oh My child, if only you could see the struggle I see My people allow. They lead such complex lives and they call it comfortable. They do not know what comfort means! That is why I have spoken these words of My lessons to My people, to help them realize what the truth is and how to achieve everlasting life. There is so much they need to learn and so much they do not even know!

Do My people now know what a blessing it is for them that My Father has allowed Me to teach them once again? The time shall pass—day by day—until they realize this gift has been taught by Me. Pray when that time comes it is not too late!

THE CROSS

APRIL 23, 1989

My dear child, what is the meaning of the cross? So many people have said there is a mystery behind the cross. I tell you...there is no mystery!

The Cross represents the way of goodness and the way to eternal life! That is why I was crucified on a cross...because I AM THE WAY! I am goodness and, through Me, you can receive eternal life.

The Cross represents Me as a symbol of goodness and everlasting life. When I carried My cross, I carried it to restore your goodness and to give to all the opportunity to have eternal life! This was very symbolic for My people because, as I carried the cross, I outlined the way! The pain I endured while carrying My cross was intense, because I was restoring goodness and paving the path to eternal happiness.

Carrying My cross was painful, but carrying your cross does not have to be painful because I have paved the path of My way.

My people become fearful when they hear "carry your cross!" I never said their crosses would be painful! The cross simply represents My way, My goodness and eternal life!

It is because I carried the cross for My people and restored goodness and carved the path, their crosses do not need to be painful. I wish today to make this clarification on the understanding of the cross!

The Cross is My Way, My Path. Because I have led the way on the path with My cross, your passage is only lightly burdened, restoring your goodness and cleansing you for eternal life.

Do not be afraid, My people, of the cross. The cross belongs to you for I belong to you and I belong to the cross, My way, My path of goodness leading to everlasting life with My Father.

Behold...pick up your cross joyfully, for it is your restoration of goodness and the paved passage. If you can grasp that I carried the cross to restore goodness and carve the path to My Father, you will realize how lightly burdened your cross is, because I carried My cross for you!

Because I had pain does not mean you will have pain, for I carried My pain for you. See the cross as freedom, as pleasure, goodness and peace—**not as pain!**

The Cross, My cross, is the way of restoration of goodness and eternal life. My way, My path, My goodness will allow you to share in My Divinity—My eternal life with My Father—My cross!

PRIDE—EGO

MAY 30, 1989

My people do not listen to Me. They are deaf to My words. They pray to Me for events to happen and, when they do, they act in disbelief.

Why should My Father allow signs from Me if, when they happen, there are unbelievers?

We have now allowed My mother all that she wishes and My people still look on in disbelief. She is the beauty of My heart. If My people do not listen to Her words, they will not listen to Mine!

Her words are of love, prayer, thanksgiving and encouragement. My words are of mercy, forgiveness, love and respect.

If My people do not wish to hear the truth from their Lord, God, whose words would they live to hear? Which god? The one they create?

You people cannot handle all I wish to give and teach because of your pompous ego and pride. When you do listen, you do not obey!

Do not wonder why your Lord, God, does not appear to all! Practice your faith. Believe in Me and allow Me to love you. Follow Me. Live My way, not your prideful way!

PLEASE BEGIN, MY PEOPLE. ALLOW ME TO
FILL YOU WITH TRUTH AND HAPPINESS.

PATIENCE

MAY 31, 1989

Patience is a virtue!

My people want, want, want. They need patience to prepare to receive. You must prepare and be patient in your preparation to enter My Kingdom.

You cannot have as you wish at all times. My people want to enter My Kingdom, but they are not patient in their prepaation to enter. You must prepare to enter My House.

In your preparation, you must accept that which I bring you, be at peace and, most certainly, be patient!

There is a purpose, Mine and the One Who sent Me, for everything!

Take one day at a time. Be patient, be loving, be open-hearted to accept My graces and pray.

Pray for My strength to endure. Pray for true holy preparation. There is no need to know how you can prepare. If you pray, as I have mentioned, all shall be given to you in accordance to Our wish and the Holy Spirit shall guide you!

Patience is a holy virtue, yet so many of My people do not pray for patience. IF YOU ARE PATIENT, YOU ARE OPEN-HEARTED BECAUSE YOU ARE OPEN TO CHANGE WITH ACCEPTANCE!

If you choose not to be patient, you wish to live in accordance to your agenda, not Mine. This will only frustrate you in your journey.

BE AT PEACE, RELAX IN MY SPIRIT. DO NOT ATTEMPT TO CONTROL.

The grace My people need to accept in their preparation is patience. All with time and patience, for the human heart is slow to change. All that you receive is for a purpose.

PATIENCE: ACCEPTANCE WITH AN OPEN HEART OF THAT WHICH MY FATHER AND I SEND YOU!

CHASTISEMENT

JUNE 5, 1989

When you, My people, open your hearts to Me and allow Me to love you, you are allowing My Father to restore the beauty initially created by Him in you! You cannot imagine the beauty created by Him!

My people, DO NOT WAIT FOR THE CHASTISEMENT FOR THE BEAUTY OF MY FATHER TO BE RESTORED! If you will allow Me now to dwell in you, the beauty of My Father will be recreated.

Do you not realize the power you have through love, faith and prayer? Through faith in Me and the One Who sent Me, trust, love and prayer, all beauty and peace can be reestablished, preventing chastisement! All goodness can be restored if you open your hearts and believe and practice what I teach you.

The chastisement shall be a result of misbelief, lack of love, lack of faith, lack of respect and from the lack of your mercy!

I tell you, if you change your hearts and live what I tell you, goodness, purity and beauty can be restored by destroying evil now.

YOU HAVE THE POWER TO DESTROY EVIL IF YOU ALL FOCUS ON ME AND ALLOW ME TO LIVE IN YOU. YOU CAN PREVENT THE CHASTISEMENT FROM MY FATHER!

Prayer and faith in Me are powerful tools. Begin using these gifts and allow Me to love you. You will see the change, I promise you! Please, just try as I have asked you.

I tell you, the chastisement will come from your not doing the wish of My Father! It will be because you have placed restrictions on the goodness of My Father, Who is all good and the Creator of all beauty.

I tell you now, that the majority of My people of this world do not listen or hear My words of truth! They do not believe in My words and choose whom to love. Because they do not believe, they take it upon themselves to control according to their desires.

I am here to tell you, My people, that you can prevent the works of the evil one and destroy him now by loving.

I am here to tell you, My people, that so much good and beauty can be restored through prayer.

I am here to tell you, My people, that wars can be prevented through prayer. Freedom and peace can BE through prayer.

> PERSEVERE, HAVE FAITH IN ME, LOVE ME BY LOVING AND RESPECTING ONE ANOTHER. OPEN YOUR HEARTS, HAVE MERCY AND PRAY. THIS IS THE KEY TO PREVENTING THE CHASTISE-MENT, DESTROYING EVIL AND RECREATING THE BEAUTY OF MY FATHER!!!

Do not think, My people, that if the majority of the people in the world in which you live do not believe, there is no hope! This is not the attitude to take. There is hope!

I tell you, you can prevent what is to come if you begin now to love and have mercy for one another.

> YOU DO NOT REALIZE HOW MUCH POWER YOU HAVE THROUGH ME!

These are not words of hopelessness, but words of victory and peace. BEGIN! TRY! PRAY! See beauty recreated before your eyes.

Anything is possible through love, **anything and everything.** Peace to you, My loved ones. . . Peace!

REST

JUNE 8, 1989

My people, know that in your journey with Me, you need rest. Do not try to do all things at one time. Walk with Me at My pace! All will fall into place if you will allow me to dwell in you. Do what I ask of you...nothing more.

I have asked you to love one another. Be loving people, respectful people and merciful ones. Allow My mercy to flow through you out onto one another.

My loved ones, you who desire Me to dwell in you and have invited My love, do not try so hard! Be at peace and rest. Do not run ahead of My pace. You desire to please Me and, in so doing, are doing far more than what I ask. This will only tire you.

Pray, love and be happy, filled people. Give everything to Me. Allow Me to lift your burdens. I shall care for you.

Love Me by loving one another. Love all...not selected ones of your choice, and be patient, My people. All with time according to My Father's wish. Be patient!

Do not live for momentary pleasure! Live for My treasure of everlasting life. Practice what I teach and you will begin to live in the holiness of My oneness.

Do not only read what I say to you. Practice My words! My words shall take you all out of exile.

Live in Me, practice My Way, follow Me! Rest in Me and live one with the Trinity! Peace to you.

TO HIS PEOPLE

JUNE 11, 1989

Come all and give fervant thanks to My Father.
He is Creator of all goodness!

> "Oh Glorious One on high, exalt your people.
> Bring them Your peace and Your everlasting love.
> I bring them to You, Oh Gracious One.
> Have mercy on them as I have mercy on them.
> They are Our beloved people."

These, My dear people, are the words I pray to My Most Glorious and Good Father. As you continue to give Me your hearts, I continue to present you to Him, asking Him to restore peace through His Divine Goodness and highly exalt you as His holy people. My Father does not deny Me My people. Please, do not deny Me to bring you happiness and peace!

MY FATHER LISTENS TO ME. WON'T YOU, PLEASE, MY PEOPLE, LISTEN TO ME AND TRUST ME?

There is nothing I would not do for you, My people, for I am good and loving. Please learn and begin practicing what I teach you. It will be your salvation!

These are words of encouragement today, My beloved ones. Take heed and pray. All goodness shall be given to you.

Times of ages change, the human heart changes, but I, your Lord, remain the same and continuously pray words of salvation to My Father for you, for **I AM YOUR FORGIVING LORD!**

CLEAR CONSCIENCE

JUNE 12, 1989

My dear people, do not be uncertain in accepting the truth of My mercy! Do not be uncertain in using the gifts I give you. Uncertainty will only cause a road block in your journey with Me, and lead to a weak conscience. Uncertainty will lead you to doubt in My truth.

It is good to question, My people, do not be mistaken. it is not good, however, to allow your uncertainty to eat at the inner core of your conscience!

Be certain of My mercy and My love, which shall flow out for all who desire me. If you allow me to love you and allow My mercy to flow on to you, you will have a clear conscience. A clear conscience is required for My mercy to flow out from you!

Do you have a clear conscience?

Are you filled with anger?

Have you sought reconciliation with your fellow brothers and sisters?

Have you allowed Me to love you so that you can have a clean conscience?

Are you ready to receive My mercy?

Are you ready to allow My mercy to flow through you?

These are not words of intimidation, My people, but words of love for your inner growth! I love you so much, My people! The intensity of My love for you cannot be measured.

I wish for you to live in My mercy. To live in My mercy you must live with a clear conscience.

These words on a clear conscience and unquestionable trust in Me are not to make you feel uncomfortable but to teach you the tools to receive guaranteed salvation! They are to awaken you. You do not realize how powerful the gift of love in itself is for salvation.

Couple the gift of love with the gift of My mercy and you shall radiate in My holiness! This is all possible, My people, and it is yours...for I am yours!!

Look at yourselves, your conscience! Reconcile with your brothers and sisters! Accept my mercy with certainty and receive My peace. You will be ever so happy because I will be in you, and I am happiness. **I am your God of love!**

REDEDICATION

JUNE 13, 1989

My dear people, I, your Lord, wish to make known to you My rededication to you! On this day I, once again, affirm my love for you by giving you My heart!

Through My blood you shall be sanctified.
Through My Spirit you shall be glorified. A day of renewal is at hand when the people of God shall no longer suffer, but rejoice! You shall all rejoice in my goodness. Continue to pray, My people, and live My Gospel words. They are for your renewal and salvation.

Blessed be you who suffer. . .for My Kingdom shall be yours. Blessed be you with torn hearts. . .the blood of My heart shall rebuild you and strengthen you as children of unquestionable faith. All, who suffer because of Me, shall not suffer in the next life! Your sin is expiated!

To suffer is a blessing from Me. Rejoice and accept. Your reward shall be great.
So today, My people, know that I, your Lord, am with you and consecrate My heart to you. Will you give Me your hearts?

Together we will be united and bonded in the oneness of My Father and Holy Spirit. All that I have, I give you! An affirmation of My love is the confirmation of the forgiveness of your sins!
Come to Me and be cleansed, refreshed and glorified in My Holiness. Come to Me, My children. . .Come! Allow Me to purify your tender hearts.

LOVE

JUNE 19, 1989

My dear people, what is love? Do you know?

Love is allowing My compassion and mercy to flow through you.

Mercy is allowing the compassion of My love to flow through you!

To love is to have mercy.

To have mercy, you must love.

I have said this world cannot survive without love. Without love all existence will cease because, without love, the soul withers.

If you wish to be My people, you need to know what love is according to My Father's standard. If you wish to be My followers, you must love.

Love is not an emotion! It is a gift of My Divinity. It is the gift of Myself. It is allowing Me to encompass your total being, because I am Love!

If you allow Me to dwell in you as your God of love, then, not only will you receive My compassion and My mercy, but My compassion and mercy will flow out from you.

If you ALL allow My love to flow through you, is that not ALL the different members making up the one Body of Christ? Is that not all My people drawing to the center of the Body, the oneness of My Body, the Trinity? It is necessary for ALL TO LOVE.

When one member of the Body loves and the other does not, the Body becomes weak and suffers. You all belong to Me and all need to allow Me to love you and build strength in you so that all members of the Body can be united with one Body of Christ!

I tell you, My people, you cannot survive without love. Your existence will cease and beauty will be destroyed. When existence is threatened, wars are created as hope for survival! This is truth, My people. Trust in Me and believe My words.

BEGIN TO LOVE BY FIRST ALLOWING ME TO LOVE YOU!

My compassion and mercy will then flow out from you. Beauty will be recreated and happiness, goodness and purity will be restored! Then you will have peace, because you will have allowed Me to give you peace!

MY WORDS

JUNE 20, 1989

My dear people, you wonder why I say the same words over and over again!

I tell you, I wish to teach you other important tools for your salvation but it is you who prevent Me. If you cannot grasp or begin what I teach you now, you will not begin to practice what I wish to teach you in the future!

I repeat over and over again the basic core of peace and your salvation. When are you going to begin to practice My words? When are you going to open your hearts and allow Me to love you? WHEN?

I have not humbled Myself to teach you words of truth given to Me from My Father so that you can leisurely read them as a pastime! **I Am here for you, My people...to save you!**

Take seriously My teachings. Begin to practice My words of love so that I may continue to teach and restore your peace. Receive graciously My words for, I tell you, the time will come when you will no longer hear them! They are for your salvation! They are for your life, not your death!

So do not say, My people, the same message is reiterated over and over again. When you begin to do as I have requested, My Father will allow more to be given.

I am here to save My people—to desperately try to save them! But they are not listening to Me nor allowing Me to save them. Bring to Me this week My people in prayer, My child. I will listen and be comforted.

LISTEN, BELIEVE, COME

JUNE 21, 1989

My child, I tell My people to come to Me and receive goodness, but they do not come. I tell My people that they shall have life, but they do not believe. I tell My people that, if they give Me their hearts and allow Me to love them, they shall have everlasting life and dwell with Me in My Kingdom. They do not listen and remain afraid. What little faith!

Do you think I came into the world to be crucified for pleasure? I came to save you! I died for you so that your souls would be with My Father. They do not listen.

I tell My people. . .have faith in Me and gain my power of love. They question the truth. They question because they do not see. They have little faith.

They think I do not notice them. They think I do not hear their prayers and listen, and they continue to suffer. Such little, little faith.

I say, first seek the Kingdom of God.
Live in My faith and allow Me to give you My peace.
Then and only then will you not suffer.
Come into My loving arms at all times.
Do not come to Me only in times of your need.
Come to Me at all times. . .seek me at all times.

My people, humble yourselves to Me as I have humbled Myself to you! If you believed I died for you, then you would have faith in Me at all times. Whether you believe I came as a prophet of God as My Jews believe, or as Son of Man, you would believe in the Kingdom of My Father and live in faith! I tell you, you do not live your lives in faith!

First seek Me, your God.

I wish to tell you, My people, that I listen to you and **it is I** Who suffers much pain when you live with such little faith. I suffer because you do not believe that I have reserved a place for you in My Kingdom.

If you truly believed, you would have no fear. You would not be afraid to die! You see death as death. . .not life! What little, little faith you have! If you think I was crucified once, you are mistaken! I die continuously for you because you continuously crucify Me! Soothe My wounds with your love and have faith in Me. If you have faith in Me, you have faith in My Father. If you have faith in My Father, you have faith in Me. Know the truth. My people! BELIEVE! Live in My faith of everlasting goodness.

My people, I wish to tell you that I have not chosen this child because I love her more than you! There is no favoritism in My love. She seeks first the Kingdom of God. She brings to My Most Compassionate Heart daily prayers for **you.** She pleads for your salvation and I listen to her. I listen to her because she listens to Me!

I tell you...long after My mother is no longer permitted to come to you, I shall continue to speak to her because she listens to Me.

Why do I mention My servant? She works, as you, and lives in My sacrament of love and marriage, as many of you. Why do I mention her? Because I wish for you to know how very extraordinary YOU ALL ARE and special to Me! I LOVE YOU ALL. I tell you this so that you will know that you can live in Me.

If I listen to her, who is very ordinary, would I not listen to you if you gave Me your Heart? I tell you, My children, so that all of you will receive the great reward which awaits you if you will allow Me to give it to you!

Do not hesitate any longer, My people, in your love for me. I wish for ALL souls to be with Me...NOT ONE, BUT ALL!

I have reserved a place for you! Please do not hesitate any longer. Come to Me.

MY PAIN FOR THE DESIRE FOR YOUR LOVE FOR ME, IS IMMENSE. Please stop crucifying Me by allowing Me to love you!

CHALLENGE

JUNE 22, 1989

My people, when you are verbally challenged with the truth of My goodness, I ask that you do not debate. There is no need to debate over what is fact.

If you wish a challenge, live your lives in My peace by practicing My ways. A challenge is not only carefully selecting your words, but putting your words into action!

So many of My people are quick to verbally respond, but slow in living out their words through their actions.

My people, live your lives with a conduct of goodness and purity. Practice and live in My ways of truth. This type of challenge will only seek favor for you from My Father, because you will be living in Me and in favor of Me.

Change your standard practices and live in favor of Me through the purity of your actions. This is the challenge and all who listen to Me and live in My love, My mercy and My peace, shall win favor in My sight and My Father's.

Challenge: putting into action the words of My truth, purity, simplicity and faithfulness. Peace to all of you.

PRAYER: PRIVATE & COMMUNAL

JUNE 23, 1989

You have heard My gospel words: "When you pray, pray quietly and privately in your room to My Father, and He shall reward you." It is the truth!

Pray privately to me and I shall answer you. Do not seek attention in your prayer. Do not boast for the glory of God by seeking attention in your prayer. Pray privately to Me and I, Who hear your most private intentions, shall grant you accordingly. Those who pray continuously, and privately, trust in Me and believe I hear them. I tell you, they shall be rewarded.

Community prayer brings great glory to My Father and

should be continued. I am speaking of true devotion to My Most Sacred Heart by praying to Me where no one can notice your actions other than Myself and My Father.

You do not realize how you are glorified tenfold in Me when you pray privately and continuously. Why? Because you are confident that I, your Lord, am hearing your prayers. It is true faith and trust and I shall grant your request according to your most intimate happiness.

Praying privately to Me in your room does not mean that you are to discontinue community worship or stop receiving the gift of My Body and Blood. My people, you need community prayer for your strength and support through the love of one another.

I am speaking of additional prayer—one of intimate privacy and great glory. If you truly are My follower, you will not seek fame through prayer or attention. You would seek humility, purity and knowledge of My wisdom.

When you pray alone to Me, it is you and I, heart to heart! Many of My people cannot do this because they are uncomfortable with themselves and have little self acceptance. If they are uncomfortable praying privately in their rooms to Me, how can they receive My comfort and peace? How? They would not be allowing Me to love them!

When My people are of this nature, I tell you, it is because they are afraid of the truth with which they would be faced and afraid of change.

There is so much turmoil in your world . . . high pace, stress for success and happiness. I tell you, for My people to sit quietly and pray privately to Me is infrequent and awkward.

Pray to Me, My people, in the comfort of your homes. I shall give to you many blessings. I shall take away your feelings of discomfort. Do not seek attention in your prayer from other people. Seek attention from Me.!

I shall grant you the peace you seek.

FORGIVENESS

JUNE 26, 1989

My child, there are so many of My people who have so much difficulty forgiving their brothers.**

There are many who are filled with so much anger that they cannot forgive! To forgive, My people must have the desire and the willingness. Those who do not forgive their brothers cannot forgive themselves.

If you, My people, cannot forgive yourselves, how can I forgive you? If you cannot forgive your brothers, how can you say you love your Lord God with all your heart? It is not possible for evil to exist with good.

I am Good! If you love Me with all your heart and allow Me to love you, there would be no doubt in your minds to forgive and reconcile with your brothers. You would love your brothers with all your heart.

Tell Me, child, if My people will not forgive their fellow brothers and themselves, is that not passing judgment? When you do not forgive yourself, you are judging yourself! When you do not forgive your brothers, you are judging them according to your standards. I tell you, you cannot love Me and hate your brothers! You cannot judge others without first judging Me!

If it is necessary for you to commence the reconciliation process with your fellow brothers. . .then do so! Take the first step! Seek courage and strength from Me, but do not delay. Each moment you delay, you deny yourself My grace of freedom and peace.

I tell you, if you wish to be glorified in Me, you must reconcile and forgive. My people, do not take lightly My words on forgiveness and reconciliation. I tell you, it is better for you to forgive and reconcile with your brothers than to burn in the flames of Gehenna!

Step down from your thrones, My people. Do you actually think you can have everlasting life without forgiveness?

Allow Me to destroy your pride so that you can live in freedom and happiness by forgiving. Stop thinking you are far better than your fellow brothers or it is belittling to forgive! There is no one of more importance in My eyes. If you cannot forgive without expectations, you cannot have a pure heart! You remain with a heart that is stained!

I wish for you, My people, to have a happy, joy-filled heart. **It is your choice!** It is you who must have the desire and willingness to forgive and do so! I cannot forgive you unless you allow Me. You must forgive yourselves and your brothers before I am able to forgive you!

**Brothers is meant by Our Lord here as both male and female gender.

TO BE A DISCIPLE

JULY 8, 1989

My dear people, I grieve for your sins because of My great love for you. My grief pierces My heart because of your sins. Begin to live pure lives.

Be conscious of your thoughts and words spoken from your tongues. The sin you commit is a result of your impure thoughts and careless words. Your actions reflect your love for Me.

I tell you that you cannot love Me at moments of your desire and call that love! You cannot love Me when you choose who to love and who not to love. LOVE ALL!

Do not hate your brothers—love them. Your actions are to reflect your holiness in Me. This is how you can decipher My true followers.

My people, please deny yourself your personal desires and follow Me. Live in My ways. Do not be holy on the surface! Be holy within. Allow Me to live in you.

A true disciple will deny himself and joyfully carry his cross for his cross is his salvation. I tell you, all of you, My people, that your personal desires will not grant you salvation! **Only I, your Lord, am the way, your truth and your source of life, granting everlasting salvation.**

Begin by making the effort, by carefully selecting your words,

words of love and comfort. Be aware of your slandering thoughts and replace them with pure non-judgmental ones. Invite Me to purify you and you will be like newborn babes.

Realize, My dear ones, how often you judge your brothers and yourselves. I tell you, the measure you use to judge your brothers will be used to judge you by My Father. You can prevent your judgment by putting an end to the judgment criteria you have established.

Be pure, holy people. Be My people of peace. Stop your arguments, stop judging one another. Harbor pure thoughts and have your actions speak for you. Live in Me by allowing Me to live in you and make you holy people.

Go now in peace, My peace. This is all I wish to say to you this day.

BLESSED MOTHER

JULY 10, 1989

My dear people, this day I, your Lord, wish to talk to you about My Most Blessed Mother. **She is the Queen of Heaven.** The angels prostrate themselves at her most holy feet pleading with her to command them! She is the purity of My Heart.

Devotion to My mother is having devotion to Me. I listen to her and grant her heart's desire. Her prayer is pure. Her desire is for all to seek the Kingdom of God. Her desire is service to Me and My Father. We do not deny her. Pray to her.

It is through My mother that you are brought to Me. She purifies you and offers you to Me.

When you pray, renounce your own spirit and invite the purity of My mother to lead you to Me! She is the Queen who has remained silent at her request. Now it is time for you to know the importance of My mother. All the angels sing at her feet and proclaim her goodness. Her prayer is so pure that We always grant her requests.

Seek Me through My mother. Pray to her with all your heart. Obey her! If you desire Me, you will desire and honor

My Mother. She is the purity of My Heart. There is nothing I shall keep from her.

I honor her. My Father honors her, and all the angels pray to her that she might graciously command them to work in her honor.

Do not take lightly the holiness of My Mother, My Queen of My Kingdom. If you wish to dwell in My Kingdom, honor her; seek her purity, goodness, humility and meekness. I will not deny you if you do not deny My Mother. Her wish is to save you by purifying you and bringing you to Me.

Praying to her honors Me because, when you pray to her, you are praying to Me! **Know the truth, My people.** My Mother, the Most Blessed and Pure Virgin is your Mother and Queen of Heaven. Honor her and you will be honoring Me. Devotion to her is devotion to Me.

PERSEVERANCE

JULY 17, 1989

My people, I continue to ask you to live your lives in My goodness. I continue to teach you to be kind to your fellow brothers. I teach these words to you because, in the world in which you live, there is little kindness and little goodness. If you practice what I tell you and persevere, you will notice changes.

Because of the evil ways in which many live, there is little trust in Me and no perseverance. Please persevere, My people, as you allow Me to change your bad ways to reflect My way of goodness.

Today, many of My people want results quickly. I tell you to have patience and persevere. All will be answered in accordance to My plan and desire. Trust in Me. Live in My goodness and persevere!

I speak to you about perseverance because you ask of Me your heart's desire, but are impatient in waiting for your answer. All prayers are heard...please persevere.

When I do not tend to your needs immediately, you question whether your prayers are heard. There have even been many of you who have said that, "Our Lord heard my prayer, but He is upset with me and no longer cares for me!" My dear ones, this is not the case.

If you truly believe in Me and trust in Me, you would know that all things happen for a purpose in accordance with My desire, which is for your happiness.

Whether you think it is for your happiness or not, I tell you, everything happens for your good! All prayers are answered in accordance to My timetable, not yours. I tell you this so that you, My dear loved people, will persevere in your journey with Me.

Stand firm in your faith and trust whole-heartedly that you are cared for. Do you give a child candy every time he asks for some? What happens should you give a child candy as soon as he requests some? I know what is good and pure for you, My dear people. I know exactly what you need as you journey with Me.

Everything happens for a purpose in preparing you to share in My glory and to dwell with Me. You are molded into perfection so that I may present you to My Father in purity.

Remember, your lives in this world are short compared to everlasting life! Therefore, My people, persevere! Continue to be kind to your fellow brothers and sisters and never stop trusting in Me.

I am the way to your happiness.

PERVERSITY

JULY 22, 1989

My people, what is perversity?

It is a blindness of the heart and destruction from your evil thoughts. Your hearts are blinded to goodness and perversity is destroying your happiness.

Remember, **I am your Lord God** and see your darkness and your secrets, which you try to hide from Me! Remember, I know the deepest incentives behind your thoughts, which dwell in your souls. Remember, I am your potter—not your clay! Do not try to hide your thoughts from me. Do not be secretive.

It is My goodness and My Divinity I wish to share with you as I have said over and over again. I wish for you to be beauty filled people with your own character, personality and style of love but, My people, do not fool yourselves! Do not play games with your emotions and deceive yourselves with your evil thoughts.

Seek Me, My people, do not hide from Me. Many put on their masks of true devotion by their routine observance of Me, but secretly lack the true love in their hearts. So many give thanks and worship to Me with their lips, but not with their hearts.

My people, stop being blind and persevere! It is the blindness of your heart which leads to your perversity. Know the truth, My people, accept it and change!

You cannot hide from Me! I tell you, you are only hiding from yourselves and denying yourselves true love, happiness and peace.

Perversity and blindness of the heart, which leads to evil, are false and empty thoughts carried out in action!

SEEK THE KINGDOM

JULY 24, 1989

My dear people, do not seek glory for yourselves. I tell you if you do not first seek the Kingdom of God, your prayers are in vain and you are seeking your own glory.

I have told you that I shall glorify you in My Kingdom but, in order for you to receive My glory, you must seek My Father's Kingdom and allow Me to be one with you. Then and only then shall My glory be your glory!

Pray with all of your heart and trust in Me. I tell you, you do not fully trust in Me. As soon as something happens in your life which you interpret as a trauma you do not trust but live your lives in stress—a stress you create. Trust in Me emphatically. Accept what I bring you. Everything is for a purpose...a purpose to strengthen you and prepare you in faith for My Kingdom.

My people, you must discontinue your critical analysis of yourselves and others. Some of you say one is a messenger of God and the other is not.

I tell you, never discredit My words given to My messengers. Please, stop creating your own conflicts. When you discredit, analyze and question the authenticity of Our words given to Our messengers in your arrogant, authoritative manner, you are discrediting, analyzing and questioning Us!

Be happy, filled people and simply accept what We bring to you. I assure you this will strengthen not only your faith, but bring you your glory! The glory of Me, being one with you.

Thank you for accepting the truth, My people. Know My Kingdom is your kingdom, if you seek it first, above all things!

ARMOR OF LOVE

JULY 28, 1989

My dear people, in the world in which you live, it is necessary for you to put on the armor of My love! Every day invite My Spirit to live in you by putting on My shield, My armor of protection, and walking in My love.

This is so very important and you will be noticed as Our children of God, Our children of goodness. Those, who wear My Father's shield, are protected forever!

Daily, dress your attire spiritually with My armor of peace, love and protection. Be the army of God!

My Father shall tend to your needs. My Father shall protect you and comfort you with His love. My Father shall exalt you for you will have My armor on, ready to battle for the sake of love and goodness.

I wore My Father's armor and now invite you to wear My armor. As I was exalted, so you shall also be, for none shall be left behind! My armor, the brand mark of My Father, is your spiritual attire of love!

SHARE MY WORDS

JULY 29, 1989

My dear child, so many of My people are so secretive.

They are friendly in order to find out as much information as they can, which they are seeking, and then do not share any of their resource information with any other people, other than a select few.

The information they are seeking is the information I have revealed to My messengers. They are seeking to hear My words I have spoken through My messengers, but they do not share My words with others.

Instead, many put their mask of superiority and importance on! They think they are better than their neighbor because they know something their neighbor does not, but they will not share either. So many of My people feel rejected because of this type of arrogance.

I tell you, **it is not I who reject My people.** It is My people who reject their fellow neighbors because they think they are more superior—a falsified importance created by man.

My dear people, do not live your lives as if you know a great secret and are too important to share or reveal your knowledge to your fellow brothers and sisters! Do not be secretive.

I share My words with you to teach you and for you to share with one another. I am not a secretive God, and if I do not keep My words from you, you should not keep My words from your neighbors. They are My people!

Please, stop attempting to find out what is happening in everyone's life and then have a facade that you cannot speak about what is happening in your life, because it's a secret revealed to you from Me! That is a facade!

All of My people are entitled to know My words and feel My acceptance and comfort. When you hide what you know from your fellow brothers and sisters, they only feel rejected.

Are you more superior than they, that you cannot share My words with them? Remember, they, your fellow neighbors, are the ones you have been called to love as yourselves!

Do not be secretive!

When you refrain from sharing My words with your neighbors, despite the desire they have to hear them, you are only hindering your growth and denying yourself My love! Your neighbors desire acceptance from you.

If you deny your neighbors the dignity and acceptance due to them, My Father shall deny you, for you are denying acceptance of Him.

There is no favoritism, My people, and all your neighbors, co-workers, brothers, sisters and families are My people. All belong to Me.

If I am not a secretive God, then those who wish to follow My way cannot be secretive! Remember, I wish for all to dwell with Me and that is no secret!

If My people wish to know what is happening to you and My other children, then share what you know. Do not create any of your man-made secrets and hold them in your heart.

Remember, if you think you are superior to your neighbor, then you also think you are superior to Me and My Father, for I live in all people who invite Me!

RECONCILIATION

My dear child, when My people come to Me to receive reconciliation, I ask that they see Me in their heart. I wish for them to pray to My Spirit to guide them in what needs to be asked in forgiveness; and then, in repentance, see Me in their hearts. A true confession will result from My Spirit's guidance, and their sincerity and humbleness.

So many of My dear people are frightened or feel awkward to seek reconciliation from Me. I do not wish for any to be frightened. I wish for them to be filled with My happiness and peace.

You see, My child, reconciliation conflicts with pride! When My people come to Me in the sacrament, they feel frightened or awkward because their pride and ego conflicts with the truth. They wish to control what they say in reconciliation, the time of speaking to Me, personally.

My priests are My instruments, and, I assure you, in this sacrament, **it is I you see,** not My priest! **It is I** you are announcing your sins to, asking Me for forgiveness.

So many of My people wonder what they should say during their confession. If they would first see Me with their hearts, they would not be frightened.

Secondly, if they would then ask My Spirit to make known to them what needs to be cleansed in them, and ask for guidance, it would be given to them along with My peace.

Thirdly and lastly, My people need to humble themselves to accept the truth, and allow Me to unite My goodness and purity in them. The joy and the freshness would be so overwhelming in this time of confession to Me that they would feel reborn. It would be a rebirth, and they would be united to Me in My Oneness with the Trinity!

If they do not feel reborn and fresh, it is because they have not done what I have mentioned, and because they have denied themselves My truth by controlling what they say to Me, hiding their sins!

I wish to make this known to My people.

It is I you reconcile with, not My priests! See Me with

your hearts. Know it is I, and personally I, listening and granting you forgiveness.

My priests are My instruments. They do not label you as a bad sinner, because they also sin! They bless you in My name, and affirm My forgiveness. Please do not deny yourselves My goodness and peace. Allow Me to forgive you!

All I ask of you is to come to Me and truthfully, sincerely and humbly ask for My forgiveness.

Do not hide from Me! Be honest and come to Me, so I can make My home with you!

VANITY

AUGUST 8, 1989

My child, My people are vain people.

Better to be simple and poor than to be rich, vain and seeking My knowledge out of curiosity. Better to be rich, humble, charitable and seeking humbly My knowledge than to be poor, filled with disgust and hatred! Better not to hear My voice if you will be proud, and better not to seek My wisdom if it is for vanity!

I tell you child, My people are vain. There is no humility or self denial. My people do not renounce themselves, and ask for My Spirit to purify and sanctify them...vanity!

Woe to those who seek My knowledge out of curiosity, instead of seeking My knowledge with humility and with lack of pride.

I tell you, those who have been given the grace of My knowledge will be judged heavier than those who do not have this grace. Caution to those who have my knowledge and live in vanity, lacking my humility!

Live for an everlasting life.
Pray that you will not be tempted.
Pray for My truth to dwell in you.
Pray for humility and, most definitely, pray that your vanity

be slain!

Stop seeking exterior fortunes.

Seek My treasure internally. Your external treasures are short lived.

The body spoils and decays, but your soul lives!

The interior soul is what needs to be fed with My treasures.

Vanity and seeking external stimuli as your treasure will only kill your soul! If you wish your soul to live, then seek Me with humility and self denial. Vanity inspires the evil one, but self denial slays him!

If you wish to receive My knowledge of everlasting life, then live your lives with humility. Know it is better not to speak if your words lack humility, are full of pride, and question disrespectfully. My knowledge would tell you first to look at your own actions, and repent before My Father!

Woe to those who discredit these, My words of truth—My priests, My nuns, My theologians, My lay people.

I tell you who have received the gift of My intellect: "Beware that your pride in My knowledge does not deceive you, or distract you. Pray for humility and self denial."

Before you judge My servant, look internally and judge your own pompous actions! It is you, who have been given My knowledge, that I shall judge heavier, and more sternly! Why? Because you, with whom I have shared My knowledge, have created standards on who should receive My knowledge, and how My knowledge should be shared! Remember, **I am your Lord, God—you are not Mine!**

I choose to work in the desire pleasing to My Father. Take heed of My words. Your vanity is killing your soul. Caution to those who seek My knowledge in vain. Know that excessive desire to obtain knowledge will deceive you. This type of knowledge does not profit your soul.

Let My servants rejoice in Me, not in themselves, nor in any other person. I am your true hope, your joy and your crown. I am your gladness. I am your Lord!

DEATH

AUGUST 9, 1989

My child, **know it is I, your Lord,** who make you worthy in My sight! We must continue with another lesson. It is a lesson on death.

My people live their lives as if they have much time to pass! My people do not know the hour or day I shall come to take them. They do not live their lives in purity, good conscience or self denial. When the time comes that they will be judged, the few minutes of their earthly life remaining is lived with grief and remorse for not repenting.

How foolish the one who thinks he shall live until tomorrow. The day of tomorrow is uncertain. Prepare as if death were today!

If you live your lives with good conscience and in My purity, you would not have much fear of death. You would know, visualize and be at peace with death, as being your true life.

Do not be attached to earthly things! Do not seek to find treasures in people. Seek your abode in Me.

I tell you, your many acquaintances shall forget you! You are only a momentary necessity to many, and many shall forget you! Seek your treasure in Me.

Oh, the vanity of My people who seek success from others, only for their well being, instead of seeking the successful path to everlasting life.

I tell you, the time will quickly come, and you shall be taken away and, at that time, you shall be taken out of sight and out of mind!

Live your lives, and strive for death to find you favorable in My sight!

Those whom I find prudent and prepared shall have full life in peace.

"For he does not know what hour the Son of Man
shall come."

Live your lives in purity, and as if death were to find you today. Be prepared and repent now! Do not seek fame and attachment to earthly things. Seek attachment to Me, and acquire heavenly treasures. Your earthly treasures shall disappear, and your fame easily be forgotten. Be fearful that I, your Lord God, do not forget you!! For those who live for earthly treasures and momentary pleasures shall be forgotten by the Son of Man.

Know death is the beginning of life. Those who live with humility and self denial would be at peace with death. Those who do not live the truth of My words should fear the hour that death would fall upon them.

Fear that your soul be ready and found in good standing, for the Son of Man to make His resting place! REPENT AND REFORM YOUR EARTHLY, VAIN LIVES TO THE LIFE OF EVERLASTING PEACE!!

TRUTH

AUGUST 10, 1989

I wish to teach My people of My truth.

Truth is not seeking philosophical words about how to live My goodness. TRUTH CANNOT BE DEFINED BY WORDS! TRUTH IS THE LIVING BREATH OF MY SPIRIT.

It is putting into action prayers of mercy and charity. To speak the truth, you must live My truth, the truth of My living Spirit by being one with Me.

The philosophers gather to define truth, but their definition is only words, and that is the reason there is much debate over what is true and what is not! I tell you, that there is no definition of truth, because truth is My living Spirit.

All who are one with Me live in My truth, for they are living in My Spirit. You can have examples and explanations on how to live to find truth, but **The word truth, itself, is Me, for I am truth!**

My living Spirit is the truth for all men. How happy the man who finds Me, and lives in Me, for he is living My truth—My living Spirit which all men are united to in My oneness.

If your philosphers lived in Me, they would be the breath of My truth, and there would be no debates. When all men live in Me, they are the living breath of My Spirit, My living truth.

I invite all to be the mankind of My living Spirit.
I invite all to live in Me, and to be truth.
Come all ye, and live in Me.
Put aside your vanity and pompous acts, and live in My truth.
LIVE IN ME, THE TRUTH OF THE LIVING SPIRIT!

HOLINESS

AUGUST 11, 1989

My dear one, I wish for all My people to seek My Kingdom with humility. Without self denial they cannot enter. My people so desperately wish to be noticed they lose sight that their prayer should be one which gives glory to My Father. My people wish to be holy, but they confuse holiness with fame!

My dear people, I tell you that those who are praised by man are not more holy than those who are not praised, or are disparaged.

Holiness reflects interior purity. Any man can reflect an exterior goodness, but it is the interior purity I see to judge worthiness of My Holiness.

Those who are more noticed by your human standards are not more noticed by Me! I NOTICE THE UNNOTICED AND WEIGH THE INTENTIONS OF THE HEART! There is no superiority.

Remember, the glory of man is not the glory of God. Those who seek My Kingdom, and desire to live in My Holiness, I assist and notice!

I, your Lord, see your interior desires and intentions of your heart. If you desire My holiness, then come to Me with humility and WITHOUT EXPECTATIONS.

Those who desire to truly serve My Eternal Father without

praise or fame, shall be exalted, for these are My true disciples. They are the ones who desire to serve and give My Father glory, not only in good times, but in bad times!

If you truly seek My Kingdom to receive My holiness, you would not worry or be concerned about what others say or do! You would not be disturbed by the judgment of men, and you would not seek fame in your testimony. You would live with humility and a good conscience, which results in My peace and interiorly reflects My holiness.

Remember this, My people: **Holiness is not a virtue to prove or show to your fellow brother. It is a state of your soul!** If you are holy, you have such a strong self confidence in your love for Me that the judgment of men will not disturb you!

DIGNITY

AUGUST 12, 1989

My dear child, it pleases Me so to see how your soul is beginning to magnify your Lord. When your soul magnifies Me, your spirit shall rejoice!!

My people, you live your lives without dignity! You are complacent, and have destroyed dignity! In your age, today, My people die without dignity, because there is lack of respect and love. I want dignity to be BROUGHT BACK TO MY POOR!!

You, My people, are poor, very poor—poor in Spirit! Reach out to one another, and restore the grace of a peaceful life by treating one another with dignity, respect and love.

THERE IS NO TIME TO WASTE. EACH MOMENT YOU WASTE WILL RESULT IN YOUR LOSS.

How do you restore dignity?

Do not seek vengeance with your tongues, or be spiteful. Be free from contempt and haughtiness. Be a teacher by your way of living. Preach by your deeds of a holy life. Respect one another, and love one another with the purity of the love you have for Me!

Remember, the one who loves in purity will satisfy the hunger of many, and restore dignity. He or she will restore life where there was death, and restore beauty where there was ugliness, because of the lack of dignity and love.

Come, My people, reach out to one another without judgment. Restore the dignity of My love in your fellow brethren by being the living fruits of My Vine, the freshness and purity of beauty itself!

FEAST OF THE ASSUMPTION

AUGUST 15, 1989

My dear people, on this, My mother's feast, I wish to share with you My joy, as I celebrate in her goodness, as the mother of Humankind. Lift your voices and give praise and honor to My mother, for she is your mother, as I have given her to you.

My people, celebrate, and open your hearts to her love. Her love grants you your salvation!

Be at peace, and know I have gathered your prayers to My most compassionate heart, and shall answer them according to your intimate happiness!

Bless you, My people, My peace I give you.

MALICE

My people live with malice. Malice is spite!

My people live with spite, and in spitefulness of others.
Their words are words of vengeance and spite.

Where is the absence of this malice?

Where? I ask.

When will My people live with love and not with malice?

When? I ask.

Why do My people live with spite and hatred?

Why? I ask.

There is far too much spite and envy, and only on rare
and few occasions can My love and goodness be received.
I offer to all only happiness, but My happiness is not the
happiness they desire! They seek out a happiness to console
their malice!

My people are not allowing Me to give to them the many
gifts of My fruitful virtues. That is why I have told you that
My mother shall not be able to give new messages, because
My people do not live the current ones. That is why I tell
you My teachings shall be limited, because My people will
not grasp My teachings, and live My words by changing their
hearts.

The reason stems from their malice, spitefulness and hatred
which controls their lives; envy which dwells in the core of
their souls, envy which is the poison, the venom of death.

Why cannot My people put aside their self centeredness,
and absorb My words? I will not continue to teach if they
continue to deny Me. My people are so concerned about who
I speak to, instead of the words I speak! They criticize and
condemn the actions of others, instead of recognizing their
own actions!

My people are responsible for destroying My goodness, because of their malice. Do you not know that those you hate
and dislike identify the truth about yourself?

How many times have I said: "Do not be concerned with
how others offend you, but be concerned and prudent about

how you offend others." **These words, My people, are for each one of you.**

Stop living with malice and envy!
Stop condemning others, for it will be your condemnation.
Stop seeking attention by taking credit for My words, for this shall deceive you.
Stop living in spite and hatred.
I warn you, My people, and THIS WARNING SHALL BE THE LAST.
MY LOVE IS PURE AND UNCONDITIONAL. DO NOT CALL YOURSELVES CHILDREN OF GOD IF YOU LOVE CONDITIONALLY. DO NOT CALL YOURSELVES CHILDREN OF PEACE IF YOU LIVE WITH MALICE, ENVY AND HATRED. DO NOT DECEIVE YOURSELVES!

Know the truth, for it is you who are responsible for the destruction of the world which was once created in the beauty of My Father. Know My Father's delicate creative hands are also strong, and can destroy instantly, all evil created by you!
Fear My Father Who is your Father. Live with absence of malice, and pray for peace to reign in your hearts!

PEACE

AUGUST 31, 1989

My dear child, when people are at peace with themselves, the words of others cannot harm them!
It is only when My people can achieve their own peace will they be able to pass on My peace to others. Achieving your own peace is to allow me to grace you with this peace. When you are in the state of My peace, harmful words from others cannot destroy your soul.
I tell My people: **"seek My peace by seeking the Kingdom of God."** Then, and only then, will all be able to pass on My peace and My love.
You must first seek peace for yourself. Abandon and surrender unto Me. If you desire peace and seek it according

to your standards, you shall **never** achieve it.

Peace is a state of grace. Seek peace interiorly. Seek Me interiorly! You cannot reflect peace exteriorly without first achieving it interiorly! To receive My peace interiorly, you must seek Me, and live in My truth. You must accept Me, and abandon your control and your total being unto Me!

What is peace?

It is the reflection of My goodness, without assistance of words. IT IS A STATE OF BEING, MY STATE OF BEING. YOU ARE WHAT I AM!

If you live in My peace, no evil can harm you, no evil can deceive you. Peace fights the darkness.

I wish for all to live in My peace, but My people are filled with impatience, anger, malice, envy and hatred. Are these peaceful virtues which will fight darkness, or are these the virtues of darkness?

My child, tell My people to seek My peace, and to stop judging and criticizing other's state of being. How can My people judge who is peaceful or who reflects My image when they themselves have not achieved My peace? Tell My people to begin to seek Me themselves interiorly, and to stop observing and passing judgment on other's actions.

Only I, your Lord, know who lives in My peace.
Only I, your Lord, see the purity interiorly.
Only I, your Lord, know true happiness.

Therefore, seek My peace, each of you, for your own self, and fight darkness by wearing My shield. Enough of your harmful and vengeful words. Seek the virtues of Me, and you shall receive. Seek Me honestly. Seek Me sincerely, and peace shall be yours.

MORE ON PEACE

SEPTEMBER 8, 1989

I tell My people that in order to achieve My peace, they must seek Me and My Kingdom. How do you seek Me?

Seek Me by focusing on Me in everything you do. By focusing on Me, I can give you My peace, because I am able to dwell in you, and we become one with each other.

I tell My people: "Focus on Me, focus, and allow Me to grant you peace." Remember, it is not only achieving peace by seeking Me, but YOU MUST ALSO ACCEPT MY PEACE!

I wish to tell My people, if they truly focused on Me, the personalities and trivial idiosyncrasies of their brother would not bother them! They would know that all My children have different personalities, intellects and characters. They would know that, even though they may not understand their brothers, I understand them, their incentives, and they would be at peace because of their total trust in Me.

My peace is your freedom! My peace allows you to live in this world until you see Me face to face.

I promise you, child, by an oath of our intimacy, that all who desire Me, trust in Me and completely focus on Me, shall be guaranteed everlasting life for all eternity with Me, My Father, My Mother, My Joseph and all My Angels, Saints and Prophets.

I promise you that whoever believes in Me, trusts My words and lives them shall receive My mercy and life.

I promise you that whoever believes in My mother, trusts in her words and lives them shall live in Me, and receive My mercy and life everlasting.

I promise you that all, who pray with their hearts, shall receive My heart, and unite in My Father's Oneness.

I promise to listen to you child, as you continue to pray for the salvation of this world, because you listen to Me, and have allowed Me to be your intimate friend!

I shall not deny you, because you come to Me through My mother, and I do not deny My mother any request!

**I AM YOUR JESUS OF MERCY, MY PEOPLE.
IT IS I, AND THIS IS THE AGE OF MY DIVINE
MERCY.**

Happy the man who follows Me, for He shall have life!
I am here for you!

Hail and glory be to the Father on high, for He has allowed
this to be your Age of My Divine Mercy—the Age of My
Father's Divine Mercy!!

YOUR JESUS OF MERCY

SEPTEMBER 10, 1989

My dear children, My most beloved people, My disciples
in Christ, know that I teach you My words because of My
great love for you!

These lessons are yours, and yours to share. I will continue
to teach you, as long as you will allow Me by accepting and
living My words.

When My Father no longer permits Me, I will not be able
to share with you the treasured pathway to entering My Father's
house.

Know, My dear people, that **I AM YOUR JESUS OF
MERCY**, and you are My most beloved people.

This is the Age of My Divine Mercy, and happy are you
who willingly accept it!

I love you, My dear ones, as My Father loves you. Know
it is because of My advocate, My mother, and My Father's
persisting love that I come humbly to you.

Thank you, My dear people, for your attention. **I, your
Jesus of Mercy,** thank you.

Be at peace now, and walk with Me as merciful, loving
disciples, followers of Me and My Father!

Appendix

ANNIVERSARY MESSAGE:

My dear loved ones, On this your special day, I bless you with My holiness and loving ways. Your marriage, one to be a representative to the world, is one of purity and gentle humbleness. How pleased I am to have two beautiful children, who give thanks and praise to their Lord. How much I shall give to you. You shall receive abundantly, for it is you, who only ask for My protection and love and truth.

You shall be with Me always, as all My children are invited to be, if they would choose My path of everlasting life. You are consecrated to Me, and I to you, on this day and forever more. My mother sings for joy today, because of the family love present in you. Thank you for caring for one another, and taking seriously the call of love.

Enjoy today, My dear ones, for it is a day to remember. . .a day, when My love for you was united to the Oneness of Me!

"My dear people, these words to My children do not only apply to them. They are for all of you. Please unite in My love and love each other. Please have faith and trust in Me by trusting and loving one another in the purity of My love.

It is today I join My heart to you. Take seriously your marriage for I have joined you for a purpose. Bear children in My love and be sure to know I am with you always."

ROSARY OF GLORY

1) APOSTLES CREED

2) OUR FATHER

3) HAIL MARY

4) GLORY BE TO THE FATHER, ETC.

5) ON THE OUR FATHER BEAD SAY: "IT IS THROUGH YOUR BLOOD THAT WE ARE CONSECRATED TO YOU AND YOU TO US."

6) ON THE HAIL MARY BEADS SAY: "GLORY BE TO THE FATHER, ETC."

7) AFTER LAST BEAD, PRAY: "GLORY, GLORY, GLORY HALLELUIA. IT IS TODAY WE ARE CONSECRATED IN YOU."

The above "Rosary of Glory" is prayed on the standard Marian Rosary beads. The format and prayers were given to the Prayer Group in the form of a message of Consecration.

NOTE: In all the previous lessons, the terms "brothers" or "brethren" were identified as signifying "unity," in both the male and female gender.

Part II

Messages
From Our Lord and Our Lady

Received at
St. Maria Goretti Parish
Scottsdale, Arizona

Note:

Since all the words in these messages are
those of Our Lord, or Our Lady, quotation
marks are thus eliminated.

Introduction to The Messages

It seems that whenever Jesus wants to get our attention, God, Our Father, allows Him to send Mary, Our Blessed Mother. She has been visiting us in many places and in many ways, especially in this present century. Our Lady has been with us in Lourdes, in Fatima, and, most recently, is still with us in Medjugorje, Yugoslavia since 1981. Other apparitions are being reported in many parts of the world.

She has been visiting us in a special way at St. Maria Goretti Parish, in Scottsdale, Arizona since July of 1988 with "messages" of encouragement and prayer and peace, begging us to turn to her Son, Jesus, and listen to Him. These words of love have been given through two different messengers in the parish by means of inner locutions and, at times, through myself, after the Gospel at Thursday evening prayer group.

As you read both the "Messages" of Our Lord and of Our Lady, you will see the urgency and love with which they are filled. It is the same message as from Medjugorje: Place God at the center of our lives.

May the grace and peace of Jesus, Our Lord, and Mary, Our Mother, be with you all.

Fr. Jack Spaulding, Pastor
St. Maria Goretti Parish
Scottsdale, Arizona

Messages From the Blessed Virgin Mary Given Through St. Maria Goretti Parish Prayer Group

JULY 14, 1988

My children, open your hearts to Jesus. He wants to fill you with His grace. He wants to give you His joy and He wants your joy to be complete. Pray, Pray, Pray! Know that Jesus is real! Accept your suffering so that Jesus can heal you. Give glory and praise to my Son, Jesus!

JULY 20, 1988

My children, why are you so reluctant to open your hearts? What does it take to convince you? Why is it you must see to believe? I tell you, look within and you shall see.

My children, without Jesus you can achieve nothing. Please place Jesus at the center of your lives. I invite you to allow Jesus to make you beautiful. With Jesus you can achieve everything.

JULY 30, 1988

My children, you know that all you need do is walk in God's way and heed His commandments and you will prosper, but yet you cannot and you wonder why. It is because you will not abandon yourself to Jesus. You want to control. If you allow Jesus to be the center of your lives and accept what He brings, He will bless you and all your work, and you will prosper.

AUGUST 4, 1988

My dear children, if only you knew how beautiful you are when you pray. Much glory is given to Jesus when your prayer is from your heart. Thank you, my dear children.

AUGUST 5, 1988

My dear children, on this day nothing would please me more than for you to seek the Kingdom of God. Please pray. You are so beautiful, my dear children, when you pray. It is my wish to teach you and that you be with Jesus in Heaven. It will not be difficult. Simply focus on Jesus in all your pleasures and trials, and glory will be given to Him.

Be happy, my little ones. Jesus will deliver you from your turmoil and guide you. You need only to love, pray with your heart, be humble and keep Jesus at the very center of your life. Thank you, my dear children.

AUGUST 11, 1988

My dear children, it is my wish to help save you and for you to be with me in Heaven. Only Jesus can save you. Please pray! You believe and then you don't believe. You must fully believe to enter the Kingdom of God. Please convert. Do not pray with your lips but with your heart.

I tell you, Jesus sees everything you do and has great love for you. Please be on your best behavior. Thank you, my dear loved ones.

AUGUST 18, 1988

Oh my children, I cry because there are so many of my children who do not want to be with Jesus in Heaven. I want everybody to be happy and to be with Jesus in Heaven. Please consecrate yourself to Jesus. We invite you to total happiness.

AUGUST 25, 1988

My children, Jesus accepted His crown of thorns with love and died for the forgiveness of your sins, so that you would be able to be with Him in Heaven filled with His joy. It is important to begin loving one another, so that you will be filled with this special joy of Jesus. You will experience happiness by loving one another, because Jesus lives in everyone and by loving one another, you love Jesus and His treasures will be given to you. Thank you, my loved ones, and peace to you.

SEPTEMBER 1, 1988

Oh my children, soon you will be filled with so much joy. Please pray. Pray as you have not prayed before, with all your strength, with all your heart. Pray so that I will be able to take your prayers and answer them. Bless you, my dear children, and rejoice in the living God!

SEPTEMBER 8, 1988

My dear children, do not be afraid. Jesus, Who is living, is your shield.

SEPTEMBER 14, 1988

My dear children, thank you for responding to the light— the light of eternal life. Oh my dear children, you are so beautiful; beautiful like a growing flower and Jesus is your vine.

SEPTEMBER 17, 1988

My dear children, In today's world there are so many unbelievers. People rely on their own knowledge which they think is their source of greatness. They forget where that knowledge comes from. It brings me great pain to see children, my children, who must have proof to believe. It is like buying love. This cannot be. For love is a deep passion which flows with purity. It is through this love, purity and quiet dignity that Jesus conquers.

Please pray for unbelievers; the people who cannot be happy or peaceful because they will not surrender themselves to Jesus. The people who must see to believe, the people who will not go beyond the prayer of speaking words, instead of the prayer which should be from their heart. I invite you again, this day, my dear children, to let God dwell in the deepest, most center of your life. Jesus, Who is your source of strength, energy and fresh wholeness, awaits your love.

SEPTEMBER 23, 1988

My dear children, please trust in Jesus. Totally surrender all your thoughts and actions to Jesus and be at peace by letting Him provide for you. Jesus will never harm you and will fill you with what you need. For to trust Jesus is to love Jesus.

SEPTEMBER 29, 1988

My dear children, it is my wish for you to be happy. True happiness comes from surrendering yourself to Jesus, by opening your hearts to His words. If you will allow Jesus to be at the center of your life and dwell on Him, all your problems will be minor. Dwell on Jesus, not your problems. Pray for the Holy Spirit to guide you and lead you in all your actions.

I know you are tired, my children, but I your mother am tireless and wish to comfort you. Surrender to me and trust. I will present you to Jesus in a way which is pleasing to Him. Thank you, my dear ones, for responding to my call.

OCTOBER 6, 1988

Oh my children, with surrendering there is so much comfort. Jesus is not asking you to be any different than the person you are. He wants you to experience the beauty of simplicity. He is simply calling you to happiness by loving. Allow your love to be shared by passing it on through your words, actions and deeds. Love is the simplest, most beautiful and purest form of prayer. Jesus does not want any of you to suffer. He suffered for you. He wants you to be filled with His love and for you to live it.

Ask, my children, and you will receive. Ask with purity and simplicity. Trust like a child trusts that he will be cared for. Seek the truth and the truth will lead you to eternal life. Knock and the Holy Spirit shall be given to you to sanctify you in His holiness. It is very simple—love as you want to be loved. Live with peace and share His happiness and eternal life. Thank you, my children, for responding to my call.

OCTOBER 13, 1988

My dear children, please begin loving one another. It is necessary that you begin loving your family and parishioners so it will be easier to accept what is to follow. Return to basic principles of loving and respecting one another. Let all your daily activities and work be offered as a form of prayer to Jesus. This glorifies Him and many graces are given. Jesus is alive and He lives in each one of you.

It is time for you to share the love of Jesus with those who are struggling. Pass on your love and reach out to one another. Your reward of peace and happiness will be unmeasurable. Thank you for responding to my call.

OCTOBER 20, 1988 *(None given for this date)*

OCTOBER 27, 1988

My children, I am here because of the love Jesus has for you. Oh my dear ones, won't you please allow Jesus to put His arms around you and comfort you? He simply wants you to live a happy life. He does not want you to be any other person than the special one you are.

Please stop fighting against each other. Join your forces and fight together for God. Put the shield of Jesus on and He will bring you comfort. Thank you, my dear children, for responding to my call.

NOVEMBER 3, 1988 *(None given for this date)*

NOVEMBER 10, 1988

My beloved, Jesus is rejected by many. He has been rejected ever since He hung on the cross and is rejected now.

The Kingdom is here, the reign of God is here. It is up to you to beg mercy of my Son. . .upon you and those whom my Son has sent into your life.

In that way you will show Him that you do not reject Him. The time is short; make no mistake about it.

Be serious about your conversion, not gloomy, but serious. If you work an eight hour day then you need to work equally as hard upon your conversion. If you study eight hours a day, you need to work equally as hard on your conversion. If you are retired and have time on your hands, I beg you, don't waste it. Now is the time. . .think. . .listen. He is sending you His heart. He is sending me to you. . .listen, continue to listen. This world is causing Jesus to weep and to continue to be in agony. Pray, have mercy on others, so that my Jesus can have mercy upon you.

NOVEMBER 17, 1988

Be at peace, my dear ones, the time for your visitation has come. I love you. You have given your heart to me...I love you for that. I am so overjoyed that you love Jesus, that you have decided to follow Him, that you will try to follow Him more and more every day.

Do not fear anything. The evil one has now been conquered. I will be with you from this day on. Consecrate your heart to Jesus and me. We will be with you so that we can offer your prayers to the Father. Please give me the desire of your heart this night.

(December, 1988)

Note: * Message spoken during prayer on Thursday evening.

** Message received during prayer on Thursday evening by messenger and recorded separately.

DECEMBER 1, 1988
(part one)*

My dear ones, you pray for peace. What you need to pray for first is obedience and then you will have peace. You need to listen again to the words of my Son. He wishes to grace you with peace but first you need to obey Him. Please obey Him. He wants you to be obedient children. To obey Him, you need to listen more closely to what He asks. If you listen to His words you will obey Him and then you will have peace.

Know that He loves you. Know that I love you and I am praying that you will be obedient children to Jesus. With this obedience will come sacrifice, will come trust, will come surrender, and will come abandonment. Obedience is the first gift that you can give to my Jesus.

(part two)**

My dear children, my Jesus died for you and He would die again for you because of the love He has for you. Please begin to practice and live the words I speak to you for my Jesus.

Begin by your actions and deeds to live with peace. Do not only pray for peace, live peacefully. This world can be a peaceful one if my children would begin to live with peace. Please try. Let this peace begin with you and it will flow out onto others because they will sense it through your actions. Jesus lives and loves you. Please live His words. Thank you for responding to the call of my Jesus.

DECEMBER 8, 1988
(part one)*

My dear ones, as you celebrate the feast of my Immaculate Conception, I beg you to allow my Jesus to make you immaculate in your spirit and in your heart. If you give Him your heart, He will be able to clean your heart of all that is not of Him. Do not be afraid any longer. You give so much joy to Jesus and to me in your love. Allow Him to cleanse you of every stain and offer you as a pure gift to God our Father.

In His goodness He has given me to you. Accept this gift from Him. Come to me and I will be able to lead you to Jesus. With me it is easier for you to come to Jesus. Make no mistake, there are other ways, but they are much more difficult. He has given me to you so that I can present you to Him.

Please, my dear ones, allow me that gift, to present you to Him. Thank you for listening to me this night with your heart.

(part two)**

My dear children, I rejoice today because I, this day, said 'yes' to my Jesus as you have said yes. In saying yes to my Jesus, I said yes to serve you. My coming into the world destroyed the sin of Eve. It was I who restored the hope that you would be free of sin.

With your open hearts I can present your sin to Jesus who has conquered sin. Let Him save you. Please, He wants to free you from your turmoil. Come to me. I, pure of heart, shall purify you and present you to Him. He will be the fresh running water which will wash away your sins. Thank you, my dear ones. It is today that I say yes, again, to serve you.

DECEMBER 15, 1988
(JESUS)*

As My Father sent John the Baptist to prepare the people

for My coming, so I have sent you My mother to prepare you for My coming.

My children, listen to her as she prepares you. Be ready for My grace. Establish within yourself a place for Me, so that when My mother continues to prepare you for My coming, you will have a place in your heart for My Presence.

You have opened your heart this much. I tell you I am grateful, but there are many who have not yet opened their heart. I ask you to pray with My mother, to pray with Me to God, Our Eternal Father, for the salvation of these dear ones that I wish to save. You are blessed! My mother will show you how blessed you are. My words to you are these: "Listen to Her, because I listen to Her!"

*(MARY)***

My dear ones, the sorrow in the crucifixion of my Jesus resulted in your joy. It was in His death that you were united to Him. He invites you to receive His grace. He wishes to unite you with Him in His grace.

Join your forces and give thanks to my Son, your King! Be glad for the many tidings which are to come. Pray for His grace! He is extending an invitation to you to receive His grace. There is no sorrow with His grace. There is no pain. There is only comfort and happiness. Pray to Him, my children, and focus on Him as the center of your radiance.

DECEMBER 22, 1988
*(MARY)**

My dear ones, my soul still magnifies the Lord through you . . . now!

I want you to know how happy I am, and how joyful you make me. My heart overflows with tears of joy. As you celebrate my Son's birth, I want you to know how He loves you, and how He would die again and again for you. He gives me to you now! I will be with you now wherever you are.

All you need do is go into your heart and I am there. You have already prepared a place for Him . . . (*audible weeping here*). He thanks you (*in a whisper*), and He loves you because you love Him. And I thank you for loving me so much.

You are so dear to me. (*whispered with great emotion*). I am with you! May the peace of my Son, and His ever-present blessing be with you.

I love you, my dear ones. You do have His mercy...because you are trying to have mercy on others. Thank you for your obedience.

DECEMBER 28, 1988
(MARY)**

My dear children, I am your Lady of Joy. I am joyful because of the hope I bring of my Jesus. He is your hope, your joy. And I am here to take you to Him. Please! Pray for peace! This world will change with your prayers. If you do not pray for peace, it is sure not to come.

I rejoice because of you, my children. You have given me your heart. I come to all who give me their heart, and I am now here with you because you have given me your heart. In giving me your heart, my Jesus has given you His heart.

There is hope, my children, through your prayers. Thank you.

DECEMBER 29, 1988
(JESUS)*

My children, as My mother and Joseph presented Me to My Father in Heaven, that day of My Presentation, I have allowed her to present you to Me. Please allow her to present you to God, Our Father.

Keep My commandments; have mercy on each other. And as you have mercy on each other, I then will have mercy on you. She so much wants to present you to My Father. I have allowed her to do that. I love you with a heart that is open and that has been open since she presented Me to My Father.

When she presented Me to My Father, My Father gave Me back...not only to her...but, to the world. If you allow her to present you to My Father, He will give you back to the world. The world needs you, (*whispering*), the world needs you! I love you!

JANUARY 5, 1989
(MARY)

My dear children, thank you for coming. So many of you are responding to my call. You truly are my children, and I thank you for your prayers. I speak to you tonight of trust. Trust Jesus with all of your heart. Some of you are not yet trusting enough. Trust Him with everything. I did, and I am the most blessed of all humanity. My Jesus trusted His Father right up to the time He was poured out, and Jesus became our Saviour.

My dear children, I know it is difficult for you, but you have nothing to fear in trusting Jesus. He will not hurt you. He has sent me to you to be your model of trust. Let this be your goal for this year. . .trust Jesus with everything. You will not be disappointed. My Son is never outdone in His love. Pour out your hurts to Him. Allow Him to bless you; you who have responded and are part of my Prayer Group.

My dear ones, I, who trust you with my heart, ask you to trust me so that together we will continue to trust Jesus.

JANUARY 12, 1989
(JESUS)

You are hearing My voice and I ask you not to harden your hearts. You heard these words from Scripture. The people harden their hearts against My Father and they harden their hearts against Me. I am now coming again to you to plead with you; harden not your hearts!

You pray that you would hear the word from God, the message from God. Now that you are hearing it, you still do not believe! Harden not your hearts. . .let them be open to Me, and I will give you what you ask. . .but you ask with unbelieving heart. You test Me. I plead with you, My children, do not test Me any longer. The time of doubt is gone! The time of wondering is ceased! Now is the time to listen . . .open your hearts. If you do not, they will remain hardened, and then even I, your Lord, cannot do anything for you.

This, My dear children, is the power you hold over your Lord and God. Do not hold it over Me any longer for I want to love you and heal you and strengthen you. Listen to My words. Listen to the words of My mother, whom I send you. Now is the time, dear ones. Please allow Me and My mother to soften your hearts. You ask and ask...and do not give! Give Me yourself and then ask what you will of Me, and I can do nothing but give it to you.

I want so much to love you. Please allow Me to love you. It breaks My heart to see hardened hearts. (*whisper...weeping audible*) I died for those hearts. Give them back to Me.

JANUARY 19, 1989
(MARY)

My dear ones, the Lord is with me and, as He is with me, I bring Him to you. I give you my Jesus to love you, and to bless you, and to give you His grace. You are accepting Him, you allow Him to accomplish within you what He wishes.

I am full of grace because of the Lord's will. I offer that grace, my dear ones, to you this night. Thank you for accepting this grace; thank you for accepting His love. Because you love Him so, my love for you grows ever deeper. Thank you for responding to my Jesus. My mission is accomplished... (*long pause...then, sadly, slowly, softly*)...and now my plan (*pause again*)...can begin.

Messages From Jesus and the Blessed Virgin Mary Given To St. Maria Goretti Parish

(January, February, March, 1989.)

JANUARY 5, 1989
(MARY)

My dear children, my Jesus carried His cross for you. I am now asking you to help Him by carrying your cross for Him. It shall be your joy and your strength. Trust emphatically in Jesus. Trust Him, as He trusts you.

Rejoice in His goodness, and pray in thanksgiving for His mercy. Pray, my dear ones, Pray! Thank you for responding to my call.

JANUARY 12, 1989
(MARY)

My dear, dear children, when you allow Jesus to soften your hearts, His heart radiates with such beauty in you! When you open your hearts, Jesus unites His heart with yours. It is so beautiful, and my heart overflows with joyful tears.

Thank you for inviting Jesus to soften your hearts. He wishes for you to be the jewels of His crown. Thank you, my dear ones.

JANUARY 20, 1989
(JESUS)

My dear people, it is because of your open hearts I am slow to anger and tender of heart. When you are tender of heart, your love spreads like wild flowers. When you harden your hearts, My flowers turn to weeds.

Every day you have the choice to open your hearts or close them. As you continue to open your heart, I continue to bind special graces from My heart to yours. As soon as you close your hearts and your minds, the transmission is no longer possible. That is why you are advised to pray for the Holy Spirit to sanctify you and to open your hearts. Please, My dear ones, do not despair. Simply center on Me, and remain open-hearted.

JANUARY 25, 1989
(MARY)

My dear children, I, your Blessed mother, tell you that you are my blessed children!

Live in my Son. You, His holy people, can live one with Him in His peace. Do not see me, your mother, as more blessed than you. All, who live in my Jesus are blessed as I. It is possible, through the consecration of my Son's Heart to yours. To live one with my Son in His Kingdom, you can only be blessed, because my Son is blessed.

I, your mother, am blessed, because I live one with Him in His Kingdom. I am purified from sin, because He lives in me. If you will allow Jesus to live in you, you can be purified of sin.

He, through His love for you, is inviting you to be His blessed people, living in His peace by loving one another, and centering on Him. My Jesus is tangible, as I am tangible, and We are here for you to grasp on to Us, and live in Our hearts.

FEBRUARY 2, 1989   *(no message this day during Mother Theresa's visit)*

FEBRUARY 9, 1989
(JESUS)

My dear people, this is the time of My Divine mercy. . .Accept it graciously. Accept it humbly.

What is Divine mercy? It is the power of My Divine Love in the oneness of My Father and Spirit, flowing out from Me on to you. . .Love, which is poured out from My Heart, into your hearts.

I love you, My dear ones. Thank you for your respect and love for My mother. I assure you, it is Me you are loving and respecting, for We are inseparable. We are One, as you and I are one. Thank you, and welcome to the Age of My Divine mercy.

FEBRUARY 16, 1989
(MARY)

My dear children, I, your mother, ask you to join with me these next 40 days in denying yourself for the glory of my Son. Give your love to others. Pass on your love and your mercy. Deny yourself, so that others can have. Join with me. I, your mother, will be denying myself with you for my Son's glory.

Will you please join with me in preparation for the celebration of His Resurrection? Have mercy on me by having mercy on my Son, and love His people, my children, your brothers. Thank you for responding to my plea.

FEBRUARY 23, 1989
(MARY)

My dear children, tonight I ask you, once again, for total consecration to my Immaculate Heart. I wish to lead you on to the path of holiness. It is the holiness that shines with light, and with infinite mercy.

Consecrate yourself daily, so that your abandonment to my Son's Will may be made complete. Thank you my dear ones. My blessings and the blessings of my Son, Jesus, pour upon you this night and always.

Messages From Our Lady
Given Through Thursday Night Prayer Group
St. Maria Goretti Parish

(March through September, 1989)

MARCH 29, 1989

My dear children, with the Resurrection of my Son your purity is restored. It is this day that I dedicate His goodness to you in His purity. It is today that I dedicate myself to you. It is today I celebrate with you in preparation of His feast, the feast of my Son's 'Divine Mercy.'

It is because of His goodness and His purity that we are made pure and are invited to be His guests at His feast. Pray in thanksgiving for His goodness, His Divinity, which He wishes to share with you!

Thank you, my dear ones, for responding to His call.

APRIL 5, 1989

My dear children, it pleases me so to be able to speak my messages to you.

Know, my dear ones, that all that is happening is true! It is not your imagination! My Son wishes to save His people and you are called to be the instruments of His masterpiece.

It is like an orchestra. What beautiful music is created when all the instruments are tuned and played with precision. For all are necessary in the masterpiece of art.

You are my Son's instruments and have been preparing for the grand gala! How wonderful you are and so dear to my heart. Thank you for your obedience and constant devotion to Our divine preparation.

APRIL 17, 1989

My dear children, it is such a blessing for my Jesus to be allowed by His Father to teach you as He taught in His age. It is truly a blessing.

He has lessons for you to help you realize the truth, His truth, and the way of guaranteed eternal life with Him. Soon you will be able to read His words to you.

Please do not take lightly my Son's lessons. He wishes for you to be happy and at peace, resting in His Spirit. Know how blessed you are that He speaks to you and is allowed to teach you through the grace of His Father.

Rejoice, My dear ones, and begin to practice His ways. Thank you for responding to my call.

APRIL 27, 1989

My dear children, I, your mother, come to you this evening in hope that you will desire to grasp on to my love for my Son, Who wishes only good things for you. Love Him, my dear ones. Love Him with all of your heart. Do not be afraid of Jesus.

He is all good and pure and is your security. Love Him as He loves you. Join your hearts with mine and let us praise our everlasting King!

Do not despair; your prayers are heard! Do not panic for We are with you. Let us simply give praise to my Son in thanksgiving for His wondrous works. Join me this day, my dear ones, to thank my Son. Rejoice with me in my Son, Our Lord, for He is your God. He is my Son and I give Him to you!

MAY 3, 1989

My dear children, I love you so dearly and wish only to share my Son's purity and glory with you.

He loves you, as I, and We give you Our hearts united with Our Father. My Jesus was exalted high and He wishes you also to rise to eternal glory. Rejoice, my children, for where He is, so you shall be with Him!!

Thank God for my Jesus. Thank you God, for my Son is One with Him and He is your living God for eternity.

MAY 11, 1989

My dear children, I, your mother, wish to thank you for trying so hard to serve my Jesus. Continue to open your hearts daily and allow His divine presence to dwell in your so tender hearts. Pray, Pray, my children, for His Spirit to guide you. Center on my Jesus and you will find His truth and His peace.

MAY 18, 1989

My dear children, pray to my Jesus and He shall give to you and comfort you! Accept Him totally as your Lord, God.

Know that He can bring you happiness and peace. Trust in my Son! Trust in Him!

Be one with Him by giving Him glory and trusting in Him. Pray for peace, my children. Pray! Trust and pray for His peace.

Thank you for responding to my call.

MAY 25, 1989

My dear children, it pleases me so when you come with open hearts to give glory to my Son. It is in this action of prayer I am able to sing joyfully for you to my Son.

How happy I am this day to sing your praises to Him, Who so much desires your love. Do not despair! Have hope, for it is in hope and trust that all goodness shall be delivered to you.

Thank you, my children. Please continue in your journey with me by remaining openhearted, patient and ever so loving. Trust in my Son and you shall be delivered into His Divine hands! Bless you and be at peace.

JUNE 1, 1989

My dear children, I ask of you today not to allow yourself to drift during prayer. Pray ever so hard! Please...Pray! Pray! Pray!

Focus on my Son. See His face in your heart. My children, you do not realize the glory to be given through my Son. Please center on Him.

HE IS HERE FOR YOU...EACH ONE OF YOU.

Thank you for responding to my call.

JUNE 12, 1989

My dear children, when you pray with all your heart to my Jesus, focusing on Him, you receive His glory because you are glorifying Him. When you do not drift in prayer, my Jesus is able to dwell in you and your deepest desires and needs can be answered.

I know it is not easy for you, my dear ones, but know everything is possible through my Son.

Concentrate and practice my Son's goodness and you will grow in His holiness. You will obtain His peace, which He wishes you to have. Thank you, my dear ones, for responding to my call.

JUNE 15, 1989

My children, I am here. Thank you for inviting me.

My dear ones, I wish for you to continue to remain openhearted. I have spoken of this often because it is so important. Remember you have the choice every day to open your hearts. Please do so daily. Do not come with open hearts on Thursdays only!!

Remain openhearted when you leave for your homes and make the commitment daily to be open hearted to my Son. He will fill you with His love.

My married ones, do not argue with your spouse! Especially over your beliefs. Love, do not argue. It is your love and your actions which shall draw my dear ones to my Son. . . not your words! Love, pray, and please, I urge you, remain open hearted so that you will be prepared!

Thank you for your response to my call.

JUNE 22, 1989

My dear children, I, once again, am here with you!

Whenever you open your hearts to my Son, you can be sure that I am in your presence because you allow me.

This week, my children, I ask of you to begin fasting for my Jesus. There are many ways to fast. Go slowly and do not attempt to fast on bread and water if you have not fasted before. You are to be happy when you fast, not gloomy, and to not let your peers know you are fasting! Simply do so joy-fully. If you begin to fast and pray, I shall help you so that your fasting becomes natural. Do not fast more than two times a week! Begin trying to fast once a week.

If you cannot fast on bread and water, then delete some-thing of your pleasure and offer it to my Son. Bless you, my children, and do not fear! Offer everything up to my Son tonight and He shall purify and comfort you.

Thank you, once again, for your response to my call.

JULY 6, 1989

My dear children, I, your mother, tell you there is no time to waste in your conversion. Please, open your hearts to my Son and pray with all of your might to Him for the salvation of this world.

Do not be fearful. There is no time for fear! Be strong soldiers, faithful ones, and begin living in His purity. I cannot stress enough to you the importance of these words!

Please begin acting as pure soldiers, my angels of love. Put aside your personal desires and seek the desire of my Son. I am here for a purpose. That purpose is to bring you to Him, and to save you—only this!

Thank you, my dear ones, for responding to my call. Our peace is with you.

JULY 13, 1989

My dear children, one year ago I asked several children if they would deny themselves for my Son's glory and suffer much ridicule. They responded joyfully to His service. For one year now I have been preparing them and molding them to be the leaders of my army of which you are all a part.

You must know that these children are not more special than you, but that I and my Son selected them to carry out Our commands because of their youth, strength and energy!

Know you are all chosen and are my children, my Son's people. These children have been given symbols which you are to live by and have been given many special graces of discernment, spiritual healings, emotional healings and physi-cal healings.

In addition, one of these children has been selected by my Son as a source through which His Divine Radiance and Mercy shall flow out onto many. These children shall soon be made known to you for they are at the end of their preparation.

My dear children, know We are not asking you to change your way of life, but to change your heart so that your lives can be lived in happiness. My Jesus wishes for you to be His chosen ones. All who desire Him are chosen!

Thank you, my dear ones, and please, support my children with your love! I tell you they are working on your behalf for your salvation! My peace be with you.

JULY 20, 1989

My dear children, first always seek the Kingdom of God. Live your lives in the holiness of my Son and seek His Kingdom.

I tell you, if you do not seek the Kingdom of God, your prayers are in vain! He is the truth and all your works should be done to His pleasure. Seek the Kingdom of God first, above all.

Thank you, my dear ones, for responding to my call.

JULY 27, 1989
(JESUS)

My dear children, today I again, give you My mother. She is My Love and My breath!

I give you her because you are her loved ones, and her breath of desire. Allow her to be your love and your breath!

She is so beautiful, and is all that I am! Give her honor. When you give her honor, you are giving Me and My Father honor. Our honor will result in your glory!

Thank you for your faith in Our truth. Peace, and My blessings to you.

AUGUST 3, 1989
(MARY)

My dear children, receive my Son through His Eucharist. Receive Him and invite Him to purify, dwell and rest in you.

My children, you do not realize the power of my Jesus in His Eucharist. It is He—in physical form, my Son, your Jesus, the manna of life!

Please, receive Him and allow Him to make you holy! Thank you, my children, for responding to my call.

AUGUST 10, 1989

My dear children, this week I invite you to ask my Spouse, the Holy Spirit, to dwell in you and guide you.

All you need to do is ask Him to dwell in you at the beginning of each morning. He shall watch over you, and you shall see His wondrous works as He guides you this week in your daily lives. There is something for all of you!

PLEASE, do not forget to invite Him daily!
PLEASE, invite the Holy Spirit to dwell in you.

Thank you, my dear ones, for your response to my call.

MESSAGE FROM OUR LORD ON THE FEAST OF THE ASSUMPTION

AUGUST 15, 1989

My dear people, on this, My mother's feast, I wish to share with you My joy, as I celebrate in her goodness, as the mother of humankind.

Lift your voices and give praise and honor to My mother, for She is your mother, as I have given her to you.

My people, celebrate and open your hearts to her love. Her love grants you your salvation! Be at peace, and know I have gathered your prayers to My most compassionate heart, and shall answer them according to your intimate happiness.

Bless you, My people
My peace I give you.

AUGUST 24, 1989 (No message)

AUGUST 31, 1989
(MARY)

My dear children, once again I ask you to take prayer seriously. In these days Satan is trying to cause much harm, and disrupt your peace. Please, pray with all your heart, and take prayer seriously.

Do not speak of my messages only! Please, begin to absorb them, and live them. Remember, it is not what you say, but what you do. Prayer will bring you to my Jesus, and is your protection from Satan.

Please pray continuously, and know I cannot give you any new messages until you begin to live the current ones!

I love you, my dear ones, and I am praying for you. Thank you for your response to my call.

Messages Given Through Homilies at Thursday Night Prayer Group

(March to May, 1989)

FEBRUARY 23, 1989
(JESUS)

Children, I have risen from the dead. The Gospel has been fulfilled, and yet, there are so many, who do not believe.

It is true. . .even when My Father raised Me to life, people did not believe, and they still do not. My dear ones, you do believe. I invite you, I beg you, to show your belief in your actions.

Be grateful and hope-filled, so that the ones who are lost will come back. Show My Resurrection in your very selves, My dear ones. I love you, and I thank you for living My Resurrection. Maybe they will listen to you, and be saved!

MARCH 2, 1989
(JESUS)

My dear ones, you give Me so much comfort through My passion. Your hearts are so soft, now, that I can mold them into loving hearts. Oh, My people, the joy that you give Me this night is deep, and will last.

The only sign that you ask is to find a new life, which I constantly give you. Thank you for your comfort. Thank you for growing in your realization of how I love you. Truly, it is for you that I died. And with your love, and by your homage, I know that I did not die in vain.

When all children will be as you are, humbly, as My people, they will pray with Me to My Eternal Father. How I long for all of them. I thank you again for comforting Me. You truly are the joy of My Heart, and I love you.

MARCH 2, 1989
(MARY)

My dear children, oh, how happy I am with your openness! Each one of you here is crucial to my plan. My plan is simple. I am working to bring salvation to my children, by opening their hearts to my Son's merciful love and saving grace.

You, my dear ones, are my instruments on earth through which I shall bring glory and praise to my beloved Son and Saviour. Do not speculate as to the details of my plan. Pray that your hearts may be more open to the special graces I wish to give you, and that my Son has allowed.

Once again, my children, I thank you for responding to my motherly call. You, who have said "yes," are my joy in these days.

MARCH 9, 1989
(JESUS)

My dear ones, Moses, who was the servant of My Eternal Father, begged for mercy for his people, and My Father listened. How much more does My Eternal Father listen to Me and to My most beloved mother, when we beg for mercy upon you.

You have My Word in your heart. You have My mother's word, who is with you during these last days of Lent. Devote yourselves, My dear ones, to pleading for mercy, and I, your Saviour, Who loves you beyond words, will take your cry for mercy to the throne of My Father, and He will listen to Me, just as I listen to My mother.

My dear ones, you must continue to listen to her. She speaks for Me most tenderly. Know that We are with you. You have nothing to fear. My heart glows with love for you. I have poured out mercy upon each of you this night.

MARCH 9, 1989
(MARY)

My dear ones, tonight I must remind each of you to remain focused on my dear Son. It is true, I am here in a special way, and it is in joy that I thank my Son for allowing it.

But children, I am here to announce Jesus, and to call my children back to Him. This is what I ask of you: "live for my Son, pray to my Son, love my Son and spread His good news." In doing this, my dear ones, you give me great joy. Thank you for responding to my call.

MARCH 16, 1989
(JESUS)

My dear children, I am giving you My mother. I know that you will cherish her, as I. I know that you will love her, with all of your heart, as I. I know that you have given her your heart, as I have given her Mine.

She and I are of one heart. When you go to her, you come to Me, and so I say, again, come to Me through her. When you are weary, come to Me through her. When you need healing, she will be and already is, My Presence to you. Ask for the love that I wish to give to you, and I will give it through her. She is so dear to Me.

She constantly says to you about Me..."Listen to Him; do whatever He tells you." Now I, your Lord and Master, tell you, do whatever she tells you. She, again, one more time, is speaking for Me.

She, My dear ones, is My Prophet to you in these days, in these last days. She speaks for Me. Listen with your heart. There is nothing to fear now. Put your hand in hers, and she will lead you to Me. Be at peace, be at peace, be at peace.

MARCH 30, 1989
(JESUS)

My dear children, from this night on, I give you My mother in the form of this statue. Dedicate yourselves to her. It is a beautiful work, done by My son, Carlos, who is dear to My Heart. She cherishes you, My dear ones, as I cherish you. Know of My mercy flowing through her.

This is the time of My mercy. These years will be years of mercy and grace from Me through her. I give you truth, hope, joy, charity, strength, faith, love, and compassion. Treat them with your love. Support them with your strength.

My dear ones, I will be sending to you people who will be in need of these virtues, and who will be in need of your mercy. Give them your mercy freely.

My mother loves you. This is her place of grace. She and I are one. When you cherish her, you cherish Me. Know that as she is with you, I am with you, too. Do not fear any longer. The new day has dawned, and with My Resurrection, each of you whom I have called here this night, is reborn. Welcome, My newborn babes!

Come to your mother, represented in this statue. When you are weak, come here and she will strengthen you. When you are fearful, come here and take her hand. When you are doubtful, come here and she will lead you to Me. She is the way to My Heart.

I love her, and I love you and I give her to you. Cherish her as I cherish her.

APRIL 6, 1989
(JESUS)

My dear ones, My beloved children! I beg you, I your Lord, not to ration the Spirit that My Father gives you. Please do not hesitate in your journey. Obey God. . .whatever the cost!

I want so very much to be at the heart of your life. I thank you for your attempt.

Please, My dear ones, do not grow tired in putting Me at the center of your lives. Be bold as you live out the command that I give you, and I will be bold for you with My Father. Use the gifts that My Father's Spirit has given you, and bring My people back to Me. Please do not waste any more time. You live as if you have not said yes! Say "yes" again this night. Please, believe when I say to you, your "yes" is crucial to My plan, which is My mother's plan.

I love you, and I am with you. There is nothing. . .nothing you need to fear now. Live in My peace, and bring My people home by the example of your obedience and abandonment to Me.

I give you My mother. Know that she pleads for you constantly, and We listen to her prayers.

APRIL 13, 1989
(JESUS)

My dear ones, I am drawing you nearer to My Father. I ask that you continue to allow Me to draw you to Him. It is a joy for Me, your Lord, to present you to My Father. Continue, dear ones, to respond. Devote yourself to following My mother's call to you to pray. Pray with your heart!

As I present you to My Father, I invite you to give Him everything. Dear ones, please, keep nothing back. If you give Him everything, He will give you life forever. Thank you for your goodness and for your generous hearts. Continue on the path. Resist the temptation to wander from the path. Take My mother's hand. She will never lead you away from the path to My Father, but will be your guide. I love you, thank you.

APRIL 20, 1989
(JESUS)

My dear ones, you have accepted Me. You do accept Me, and I thank you for that. My Eternal Father allows Me to speak to you words of hope and challenge.

It is time now to put the words I speak, and have spoken to you, into practice in your daily lives. I am choosing you as My new people. As you say yes, there will be more and more that you will understand, and that will become clearer to you. I want to say to you this night, "My way is simple!"

My dear ones, you cause yourselves much pain when you complicate My way. Again I invite you to offer all things to Me, and I will offer them to My Father. Again I remind you, I have sent you My mother. Please allow her to do what she wants with you, and that is to lead you to Me, so that I can present you to My Father.

Live in My Peace. My mercy is upon you.

APRIL 27, 1989
(JESUS)

My dear ones, I am your Jesus of Mercy! I invite you to come to Me, and I, if you will allow it, will shed My mercy upon you.

My gift to you is My love through My mercy. I ask you to open your hearts and to accept this gift.

FROM OUR LADY FOR THE PARISH

MAY 1, 1989
(MARY)

My dear children, today I ask you again to consecrate yourselves to Us! I ask you to trust Us with all, and to pray from your heart.

My children, do not have any fears for We are with you. You are precious to Us! Do not give up...Pray! Pray! Pray!

My children, cleanse your hearts so that We might dwell in their purity. My dear children, trust in my Jesus. Ask my Jesus to help you, to strengthen you, to lead you to the Father. All of your prayers are heard and all are answered.

My dear children, please open your hearts. Pray with all of your strength, your will, your soul and your mind. Allow my Jesus to fill your hearts with His peace.

Thank you for responding to His call.

MAY 4, 1989
(JESUS)

My dear children, this is the seedbed where you will be nurtured and strengthened and trained. Then, when you are ready, I will send you out.

Please, children, My special ones, do not doubt Me. You are so like My Apostles. On My Ascension Day, they still doubted and were afraid. I, on this Ascension Day, remind you again, you need not fear! Please do not doubt. Your doubt hurts Me.

I do know, My dear children, what I do to glorify My Eternal Father. Please, use this time to be strengthened and nurtured and taught. I will send you out from here. My mother loves you, and is with you each step of your way.

JUNE 1, 1989
(JESUS)

My dear ones, tonight I am with you to ask each of you, "What do you want Me to do for you?"

My dear ones, why are you still afraid of Me? I will never hurt you. I want only your true happiness. Do not be afraid of Me. Please come to Me.

What do you want Me to do for you? Tell Me this night with all of your heart and I will give you your heart's desire!

I invite you again to become closer to My mother so that I can be closer to you. If you are still afraid of Me, don't be afraid of her! Come to her and she will ease your fear and bring you to Me. I do not want to be distant from you any longer.

Please allow Me, your Lord, this grace. Open your hearts to Me. I want so much to be with you and in you. That is the desire of My heart. That is what you can do for Me. I will always love you.

JUNE 8, 1989
(JESUS)

My dear ones, you are living now in the reign of My Father. It is here with you now, if you look within and begin living the love that He has offered to you through Me.

My blest ones of you, who are living the sacramental life of marriage, live it, My children, with all of your heart. It is the blessed gift of My Father and a sign of His continuing love for you. Cherish one another. Live in My love. Re-dedicate yourselves to the selflessness of My love in this sacrament.

I bless you, My dear ones, who have been called to the sacrament of marriage. As you live that love, you will be a sign to this world that has forgotten the meaning of self-sacrificing love.

If you, My dear ones, love My Father above all else, you will love one another because in one another you will find Him and Myself and Our Holy Spirit!

I give you My blessing this night to grow and to prosper, not for yourselves alone, but for this world. Thank you for saying yes to this sacrament.

JUNE 15, 1989 *(No message)*

JUNE 22, 1989
(JESUS)

My dear ones, I again, tonight, give you My mother as the new Eve as I, your Lord, am the new Adam.

You are Our children through My love and through the water which came from My side. You have been adopted at a great price. The sign that you are Our children is forgiveness.

My Father wants to forgive you. I plead for you. My mother pleads for you. My children, please begin to forgive. That will open your heart! In your generosity of love, go deep within your heart to ask forgiveness, and the grace to forgive.

I and My Father give Mary to you again tonight. Do not ignore her or her invitation to you. Take her hand again this night, and journey in forgiveness to Me, so that I can take you to Our Father.

If, My dear ones, you need a reminder of forgiveness, look upon Myself nailed to the Cross. I loved you then and I still love you! Allow Me to love you more, as you forgive more.

My peace is with you now.

JUNE 29, 1989
(JESUS)

I have had so much hope for you, My dear ones, and now I come to you and I, your Lord, plead with you...embrace your cross.

Do you think it was easy for Me to bear the cross for you? I gladly did it for love of you and in obedience to My Father. I beg you...embrace your cross in reparation for your sins.

You have no idea how your sins continue to grieve Me! I love you! Please love Me! I want you with Me. You need to make reparation for your sins.

My mother grieves for you and pleads for you. The time is truly short. I beg you...listen to Me or listen to My mother...but, LISTEN!! My Eternal Father has sent Us to you! I died in love! Please, My dear ones, live for Me in reparation for your sins and in love. I promise to be with you always.

Message to Peace Center Day of Recollection, June 24, 1989

(From Our Lord Through a Messenger)

My dear people, eight years ago My mother asked permission in a last effort to make known to My people, how much they are loved, and to ask for your hearts. It has been eight years that I have allowed her to convert you, My people.

It is because of your prayers and love that I remain tender hearted as she brings you to Me. I now have allowed My mother to continue and to be here with you. We both, together, are here in the Americas, to gather Our people in love.

Be prepared, My dear ones, for the many to come here! Be open-hearted and ready to accommodate. I am here to save and to destroy evil so all may live in My goodness and dwell in My Kingdom. It is My Divinity I wish to share with you, My jewels of My Crown. There is nothing I shall keep from you.

You are My people and many more shall come to this, My Center of Mercy! My mother has chosen her children and I have chosen My one of love and mercy! They are symbols for this world to live by. They are symbols of truth, faith, hope, joy, strength, compassion, charity, humility, courage and My one of love and mercy. See these my children, as examples for which you are to live.

As you celebrate the anniversary of My mother's 8th year, celebrate your first year anniversary! There shall be many more to come. It is not the end, My people, but the beginning! Prepare! Go in My Peace and know We are with you.

(From Our Lady...Same Day, June 24, 1989)

My dear children, my heart overflows with joy! I am with you again this day! Pray that you will be able to remain open to my Jesus...to all of the graces He wishes to bestow upon you!

My dear children, pray with your whole heart...pray constantly. Never cease in your prayers! Your prayers are heard and ALL are answered!

Thank you for responding to my call.

JULY 6, 1989
(MARY)

It gives me great joy to be with you this night as you honor my Son under the title of His Mercy. Ask Him and Our Eternal Father to be with you. My Jesus under His title of Mercy will also be here!

Come to Him, my dear ones. My heart overflows with joy at how much He loves, and how much He loves you, each of you!

Our Eternal Father has allowed both of Us to be with you. This will be a center of my Jesus' mercy for all who come. As they come, my dear ones, whether you understand or not, you are prepared to receive all of these ones. Have mercy on them, and my Jesus will have mercy on you. He is shedding His mercy upon you now. As you come to Him, do not fear to hope, for He has great hope for you!

I take you, my dear ones, into my heart this night and present you to my Jesus of Mercy with His heart overflowing with love and forgiveness for those who ask! We will always be with you until the time when We come to take you home!

Until that time, know that this is your home, because this is where His mercy and my peace dwell for you.

Thank you for honoring my Son. Thank you, my dear ones. Peace! Peace!

JULY 20, 1989
(JESUS)

My dear ones, I, your Lord, do offer you this night My comfort and My peace. The words of My gospel message are true.

My yoke is easy and My burden light, because I never give you a task, a cross, or a burden without also being there with you every step of your way!

My dear ones, **I am your way!** Allow Me to journey with you, and you will be free and peace-filled. I offer you life...My life! I invite you to accept that gift.

Come to Me as you are weary, and I truly will give you refreshment. Come to Me when you feel lonely, and I will be with you.

You give Me so much joy! You are responding. Continue to respond in love, no matter how difficult the road. I am with you, and I give you My mother, also. Take Our hand, and We will lead you to the Kingdom of My Father!!

AUGUST 10, 1989
(JESUS)

My dear ones, My dear mother is honored by Myself and by My Father because of her obedience. This obedience did not come from her human understanding, but from her Spouse, Our Holy Spirit.

I give her to you this night as an example of the kind of obedience I invite you to give to Me, and to her, and to Our Heavenly Father. Because of her obedience, she was able to pray: "My soul magnifies the Lord, and My spirit rejoices in God, My Saviour."

My dear ones, the gift of your obedience is the gift of your heart to Me. When you obey Me, I take that gift and present it to My Father. It is because of your obedience that many, many graces are being shed upon you at this place at this time, and because of your obedience, you are causing that grace to overflow on to all those who come to you!

My Father allows Me to come to thank you for your obedience. I take you into My heart again, this night, in gratitude for that gift, and I leave My mother with you as My physical sign and example to you of the obedience that is most pleasing to My Father.

Continue, My dear ones, to cherish her as she so cherishes you! You are allowing her, because of your obedience, to lead you to Me. You are allowing her, because of your obedience, to lead you to Me.

I give you My Mercy and My love.
(Hands held out toward assembly)
Live on in My Peace.
(Hands and arms extended up over assembly!)

AUGUST 17, 1989
(JESUS)

My dear ones, Our Holy Spirit has been always with you from the very beginning of your time here on earth, prompting you, guiding you, protecting you and sanctifying you.

Our Spirit was the gift We gave you, and it is the gift that I give you again this night!

Receive, again, Our Holy Spirit. **Through that Spirit I, your Lord, touch your heart this night.** Allow Me to melt your heart if it is closed and cold. Allow Me to open it, and to pour My Mercy this night upon you.

Give Me your heart, and I will take it and put it in My heart, and there Our Father will see you in Me.

My dear ones, allow this blessing to happen! Give Me that gift, so that My Mercy and the gift of Our Holy Spirit may flow to you, healing, forgiving and sanctifying.

I love you. I will always love you! I, your Lord, will never give up on you...NEVER, NEVER, NEVER!

AUGUST 31, 1989
(MARY)

My dear little children, you are my holy ones.

I thank you for your prayer, and I invite you this night to more prayer. Honor my Son with your prayer. Pray for peace, please. Pray that your heart may continue to be converted.

I see your weariness, little ones. Please, I invite you not to give up but to continue in your prayer. Prayer is so vital to me, and for your world. Don't give up...continue.

Believe me when I say, it is because of your prayer that I, your mother, am allowed to be with you in so many ways for so long a time. This truly is the time of my Son's grace.

Never stop allowing Him to work through you. I promise, little ones, to come whenever you invite me! It is the joy of my heart when you invite me, your mother, to pray with you to my Son and our Saviour, Jesus.

Thank you for your prayer and for trying so hard to love. Your attempts do not go unnoticed! Thank you, my little ones, my little holy ones! I love you.

SEPTEMBER 7, 1989
(JESUS)

My dear ones, why don't you trust in My care for you? I extend, always, My mercy and love to you.

My Father sent Me to you, not to frighten you, but only to love you. Why do you still hesitate to trust? I ask for your obedience. Is it such a difficult request?

I long for your heart. Can't you see that when you give Me your heart, I can fill it with My mercy and love? I long to do that!

I ask you, again, listen, and obey and I will be able to present you to My Father, and flood you with My mercy. I love you with all My heart. I beg you, trust Me!

THE
RIEHLE
FOUNDATION...

The Riehle Foundation is a non-profit, tax-exempt, charitable organization that exists to produce and/or distribute Catholic material to anyone, anywhere.

The Foundation is dedicated to the Mother of God and her role in the salvation of mankind. We believe that this role has not diminished in our time, but, on the contrary has become all the more apparent in this the era of Mary as recognized by Pope John Paul II, whom we strongly support.

During the past two years the foundation has distributed over one million books, films, rosaries, bibles, etc. to individuals, parishes, and organizations all over the world. Additionally, the foundation sends materials to missions and parishes in a dozen foreign countries.

Donations forwarded to The Riehle Foundation for the materials distributed provide our sole support. We appreciate your assistance, and request your prayers.

IN THE SERVICE OF JESUS AND MARY
All for the honor and glory of God!

The Riehle Foundation
P.O. Box 7
Milford, OH 45150